CHILDHOOD TREASURES

CHILDHOOD TREASURES

—⸱ Doll Quilts By and For Children ⸱—

MERIKAY WALDVOGEL

Photography by the University of Nebraska-Lincoln

Historic photographs courtesy of Virginia Gunn, Merikay Waldvogel, Mary Ghormley, and Roger Ghormley

Good Books

Intercourse, PA 17534
800/762-7171
www.GoodBooks.com

Acknowledgments

I wish to thank Wilene Smith for her help with genealogical searches and for her assistance in identifying 19th- and early 20th-century quilt-pattern sources in women's magazines; Connie Chunn for sharing her research on the Ladies Art Co.; Diane Fagan Affleck and Deborah Kraak for authenticating the Cocheco cotton-print fabrics; and Rosie Werner for identifying certain quilt-kit sources. I also want to acknowledge my patient and meticulous editor, Delphine Martin.

Credits

On the front cover: The Raggedy Ann dolls, the quilt, and the antiques in the photo are from the Mary Ghormley Collection.

On the back cover: The doll, the quilts, and the antiques in the bottom-right photo are from the Mary Ghormley Collection. The Four-Patch in Squares in the top-left corner can be seen on page 92.

Quilt photography by David Kostelnik

Design by Cliff Snyder

CHILDHOOD TREASURES

Library of Congress Cataloging-in-Publication Data

Waldvogel, Merikay, 1947-
  Childhood treasures : quilts by and for children : featuring 80 antique doll quilts from the renowned Mary Ghormley collection / Merikay Waldvogel.
      p. cm.
  Includes index.
  ISBN-13: 978-1-56148-599-4 (pbk. : alk. paper) 1. Doll quilts--United States--History--19th century. 2. Doll quilts--United States--History--20th century. 3. Children's quilts--United States--History--19th century. 4. Children's quilts--United States--History--20th century. 5. Ghormley, Mary--Art collections. I. Title.
  NK9112.W343 2007
  746.460973--dc22   2007049929

Table of Contents

Preface 3

Introduction 9

Early 19th-Century Quilts (1830s-1860s) 23

Frontier Quilts (1870s-1890s) 41

Victorian Crazy Quilts (1880s-1910s) 59

Quilt Patterns (1880s-1910s) 75

Turn-of-the-Century Fabrics (1890s-1910s) 95

20th-Century Quilts (1900s-1950s) 115

Conclusion 131

Endnotes 133

Suggested Readings 134

Glossary 135

Index 138

About the International Quilt Study Center & Museum . . . 139

About the Author and the Collector 140

Mary Ghormley, age 2

Merikay Waldvogel, age 2

Preface

This book represents an unlikely union. Two women separated by many years and miles became friends through a love of quilts and collaborated on a project neither imagined doing—writing a book about doll quilts.

Mary Campbell Ghormley is the mastermind behind the doll-quilt collection showcased in this book. She is a prize-winning quiltmaker in her own right and has been collecting full-size quilts for many years. But she never set out to collect doll quilts. She tells the story of walking into more than one antique shop and spying a doll quilt tucked almost out of sight. They seemed to beg for her to save them. "It started with one and then another," she said. "And you know, when you have two of something, you have a collection." At last count, her collection numbers 300—possibly the largest in the world—and spans more than 100 years.

As Mary's collection grew, it began to gain notice. In the 1990s, she began receiving invitations to speak to quilt guilds, women's groups, and museum audiences. She always prefaced her remarks with a qualifying statement: "This is not a scholarly presentation; it is just about my love of doll quilts. I am a maker and collector of quilts, and as a collector, I see myself as a conservator. I'm saving these quilts from being lost,

Merikay Waldvogel (left) with Mary Ghormley

destroyed, or under-appreciated." Most notably, her doll quilts have been exhibited at the Museum of American Quilts in Paducah, Kentucky, and at the Great Plains Art Museum in Lincoln, Nebraska.

Mary's and my paths crossed at the American Quilt Study Group seminars in the 1980s and '90s. She would travel from Lincoln, Nebraska, and I from Knoxville, Tennessee, to San Rafael, California, in the days before the annual seminar moved from region to region.

At one such seminar, I shared an evening meal with Mary and her husband, Roger. We were surprised to discover many parallels in our lives, though separated by 25 years and 2,000 miles. We both grew up in the Midwest—Mary in Iowa and I in Missouri. We both attended Monmouth (Ill.) College, a Presbyterian liberal arts school. Mary studied there in the late 1930s. I graduated in 1969 in the same class with Mary's nieces. At Monmouth College we were both members of the same national sorority—Kappa Kappa Gamma—I in the late 1960s, and Mary in the late 1930s. Her first job was in Chicago, where she met her husband, Roger, in the early 1940s. Coincidentally, my first job was also in Chicago in the 1970s.

It was in Chicago, in 1974, where I had my first quilt encounter—an event that changed my career path. Prior to that day, I doubt the words "patchwork" or "quilt" had ever passed my lips. Neither my mother nor my grandmother quilted, although both women did a lot of sewing for their daughters. What thrilled me about quilts then, and what continues to enthrall me now, are the fabrics and the privilege of owning a quilt that has endured through history and imagining what stories it holds. Mary can relate to this. Quilts and the fabrics they contain are a treasure to both of us—even the well-worn, poorly made, or unfinished ones. As mature, long-time quilt collectors, we look to the fabrics to help us accurately date when a quilt was made.

As my career as a quilt historian bloomed, I was invited to speak at quilt guilds and give workshops on quilt-dating. One year when I was invited to Nebraska to speak at a statewide quilt conference, Mary invited me to spend the night at her house. I'll never forget my first impression walking into her home. Quilts were everywhere. She escorted me to the guest bedroom—a quilter's paradise! Quilts were folded carefully and stored in trunks, chests of drawers, and on closet shelves. Framed miniature quilts lined the walls, and a collection of doll quilts, doll clothes, and doll beds filled the corners of the room. I knew I had found a kindred spirit.

Over the ensuing years, our friendship continued through correspondence. As I researched the pattern collectors of the 1960s and '70s, I came across her name and that of Louise Howey, both quilting teachers in the 1970s and founders of the Lincoln Quilt Guild in 1973. Mary had done extensive research on her own quilts and had built a fabulous library of quilt books and patterns. And yet, she was always quick to claim that she was not a quilt scholar. She would let others write the quilt books.

Every subject I researched, Mary had a quilt to share with me. When I was researching printed chintz medallion quilts, I combed through magazines, books, and museum catalogs, looking for the rare example. I mentioned my search to Mary on a visit to Lincoln for a symposium, and she said, "Oh, I have one of

The attic storage area for Mary Ghormley's doll quilts, furniture, and accessories.

those. Do you want to see it?" The same thing happened when I was researching kit quilts of the 20th century. Mary had even made a few herself!

In 1997, the International Quilt Study Center (IQSC) was established at the University of Nebraska-Lincoln with the acquisition of the Ardis and Robert James Quilt Collection. Mary became a regular volunteer, leading tours of the collection and researching pattern names. Whenever I was invited to work at the IQSC, I'd happily spend time with Mary and Roger.

In 2004 the IQSC announced a museum building project and plans for a reading room named in Mary's honor that would house her doll-quilt collection, research library, as well as some of her doll beds and linens. Around that time, Mary called me to request that I write a book about her doll quilts.

I was pleasantly surprised. I knew this good friend and valued colleague could write the book herself, but she wanted an "authority" to write it. I certainly knew

Mary Ghormley

quilts, patterns, and fabrics, but doll quilts were new territory for me. I remember asking myself, "What do I know about doll quilts?" With Mary's assistance, I learned much.

The 80 quilts which Mary and I selected for this book showcase a wide range of fabrics, patterns, and construction techniques. Those features made it possible for us to date these quilts with reasonable accuracy.

Mary assigned names to her quilts using Barbara Brackman's *Encyclopedia of Pieced Patterns*. Many of the titles she chose, and which are retained in this book, are simply pattern names—Crazy, Four-Patch, Nine-Patch, etc.

I enjoy using primary sources rather than a pattern encyclopedia or index, and am fortunate to own a collection of quilt-pattern source material, the core of which is the *Mildred Dickerson Round Robin Pattern Collection*. For this book, I searched for the primary sources of Mary's doll quilts. If the fabrics were late 19th-century vintage, I looked for 19th-century pattern sources—not the 1930s pattern publications that often renamed earlier quilt blocks.

To further bring the doll quilts to life, I include vintage photos of children and their dolls, courtesy of my colleague, Virginia Gunn, who willingly supplied dozens of selections from her personal collection. The children's faces, their outfits, and the dolls they proudly hold create a context for the doll quilts we have chosen.

The exceptional work of our photographer, David Kostelnik, of Lincoln, Nebraska, makes this book a visual treasure. He capably reconstructed period settings, displaying the quilts on beds surrounded by antiques. His expertise allowed for a magic we had not expected.

Merikay Waldvogel

Mary generously supplied the period antiques for the vintage photo settings. At age 85, she climbed the attic stairs every night to bring down the proper beds, linens, and pillows. Roger packed them all in large boxes sized to fit exactly in the back seat and trunk of their car. Obviously they had done this before. I set up my laptop and tried to keep pace by transcribing my quilt notes. Roger scanned dozens of vintage photos to disks. We were a well-oiled team and having fun.

I also want to acknowledge the funding support from the International Quilt Study Center at the University of Nebraska in Lincoln which underwrote the cost of the photography for this book. Dr. Patricia Crews and her staff have been most gracious in supporting this project.

I hope you enjoy this book. It is a collaborative effort between two friends with a shared passion—bringing quilts to life. Drawing upon our combined 75 years of quilt study and collecting, we hope this book adds to the body of quilt scholarship and, more importantly, that it entices others to appreciate quilts, pick them up, bring them home, and treasure them one and all.

Photography by Keller Studio,
Tiffin, Ohio, circa 1880s-1890s.

Virginia Gunn Collection

Introduction

Mamie Mantz of Pennsylvania
with her imported doll.
Photo by Maury Photography
of Tamaqua, PA, circa 1890s.

Virginia Gunn Collection

Crib and doll quilts are perhaps the most tender and personal of all quilts, treasured not only for their charm but also for the love that went into making them. Antique doll quilts, like all old quilts, connect us to the past. As do other works of art, they reflect the cultural and sociological attitudes of a particular time and place.

But why should doll quilts intrigue us? They aren't always perfectly made and are sometimes stained and needing repairs. Is it sentimentality that draws us to them? Or their apparent spontaneity? Many appear to have been made quickly with little thought given to design or perfect stitching. Mary found herself wondering who made the quilts, about the children who played with them, and what kind of dolls they had.

Mary's collection, shared through exhibits and lectures and also in this book, invites us to learn not only about quilt history, but also about women's history. The information in this Introduction follows closely the content of her lectures, in which she reads excerpts from 19th-century sources and shows period doll beds and matching linens. This extraordinary collection and intriguing historical research are to her credit.

Child-Made Doll Quilts— "Teaching Projects"

Childhood in the early 19th century prepared a girl for a major part of her life's work—sewing. In the days before the sewing machine, hand-sewing was an essential skill to learn. Grown women were expected to make all the family's clothing, bedding, and linens by hand. Sewing skills were passed from mother to daughter and from teacher to pupil. Little girls as young as three were taught to sew.

Lucy Larcom, in her 1889 memoir, *A New England Girlhood*, describes a scene from her childhood when she felt the weight of this responsibility, walking behind her father and mother into a church service:

I was a toddling thing … as they walked arm in arm before me, I lifted my eyes from my father's heels to his head, and mused: "How tall he is! And how long his coat looks! And how many thousand, thousand stitches there must be in his coat and pantaloons! And I suppose I have got to grow up and have a husband, and put all those little stitches into his coat and pantaloons. Oh, I never, never can do it!" A shiver of utter discouragement went through me. With that task before me, it hardly seemed to me as if life were worth living. I went to meeting, and I suppose I forgot my trouble in a hymn.[1]

In the mid-1800s, many dolls were manufactured in France and Germany, and were imported to the United States. These dolls were "little women" dressed in the latest fashions of the day. Baby dolls were introduced much later.

In America, in frontier outposts, children often learned to make do with very little except their imaginations. Children made dolls from cloth, rags, nuts, corncobs, sticks, and handkerchiefs. The doll's bed might have been made from leftover wooden slats, a tin can, or even a cigar box with clothespins for posts.

Although crude by today's standards, the dolls were clearly loved. A certain Edith Stratton Kitt, growing up on a ranch in Arizona in the 1880s, described her favorite doll in a diary entry: "My one great love and joy was Diggie. She was my constant companion for many years. Sometimes she was a stick, sometimes a handkerchief with a stone tied in one corner for a head…. I could always talk to her and tell her all my troubles, and she was a great comfort."[2]

Every young girl was required to learn numerous stitches, including the overstitch, backstitch, running stitch, and whip stitch, all of which coincidentally are used for making pieced or appliqué quilts. Patching, darning, hemming, and gathering were also skills to master.[3] Today, few women know any of these stitches.

Typically sewing samplers were used to teach girls sewing, knitting, and patching (see Plate 1). Upperclass girls were taught the gracious life of manners and needlework, and they went to finishing school to perfect both. Idleness was to be avoided, lest the devil found a foothold for temptation. Doing patchwork made girls industrious and instilled other virtues such as neatness, attentiveness, patience, and acceptance of repetition and routine.

Not every child found the lessons enjoyable. In Lucy Larcom's memoir, she describes frustration with making her required patchwork quilt:

Plate 1 — Red and White Sampler
Date unknown • 28″ x 10-11″ • Cotton.

This sampler contains knitting, crocheting, and hand-sewing. A practice repair to a diagonal slit is nearly invisible in the red and white striped fabric.

We learned to sew patchwork at school, while we were learning the alphabet; and almost every girl, large or small, had a bed quilt of her own begun, with an eye to future house furnishing. I was not over-fond of sewing, but I thought it best to begin mine early.

So I collected a few squares of calico, and undertook to put them together in my usual independent way, without asking any direction. I liked sorting those little figured bits of cotton cloth, for they were scraps of gowns I had seen worn, and they reminded me of the persons who wore them. One fragment, in particular, was like a picture to me. It was a delicate pink and brown sea-moss pattern, on a white ground, a piece of a dress belonging to my married sister, who was to me bride and angel in one.... I could dream over my patchwork, but I could not bring it into conventional shape. My sister, whose fingers had been educated, called my sewing "gobblings." I grew disgusted with myself, and gave away all my pieces except the pretty sea-moss pattern, which I was not willing to see patched up with common calico. It was evident that I should never conquer fate with my needle.[4]

A Four-Patch quilt in Mary's collection fits the description of Lucy Larcom's "gobblings" (see Plate 2 and page 104). It's not a pretty quilt nor well-made. Its center is all gathered up. Mary found this quilt with a card still attached: "Mama made this quilt when six years old in 1904." We will never know Mama's full name, but we do know that someone cared enough to save the quilt and label it. For Mary, this added to the sentimental value of the quilt. She had to buy it.

A doll quilt presented an excellent opportunity for a child to practice her sewing skills. Its small size made it easy for little hands to manipulate. A very young child might have begun sewing with an unknotted thread. The running stitch used to join straight seams was usually the first sewing stitch introduced to young girls. A child likely started with

Plate 2

the simplest quilt patterns: the One-Patch, Four-Patch, or Nine-Patch. Even if interest waned after just one block, one block was enough to make a doll quilt. Mary said her mother was told as a child that every girl should have made a Nine-Patch by age nine. When straight-sided patterns were mastered, the child then progressed to more difficult patterns with curved seams.

Girls were also known to take on more ambitious projects. During the 1987-89 Nebraska Quilt Project survey, one quilt owner, Edith "Belle" Sims Fraser, brought for documentation a full-sized quilt that

she started in 1919 as a three-year-old.
Her mother cut the pieces, marked the
sewing lines, and pinned it. When Belle
grew older, she learned to sew on a treadle
sewing machine and finished the top by
age six. She later quilted it in the 1940s.[5]

Adult-Made Doll Quilts— "Made with love for someone special"

Early crib and doll quilts were made
the same as full-size pieced quilts,
using squares, triangles, and diamonds
in the same fabrics, colors, and patterns.
Those made perfectly were likely sewn by
adults for children as tokens of love.

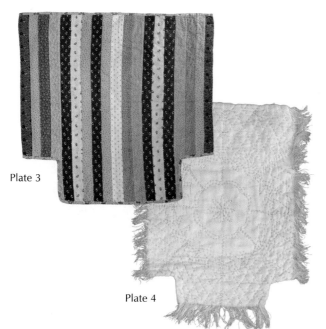

Plate 3

Plate 4

Plate 5

Half-Square Triangles (see Plate 5
and page 101) must have been made by
an adult. The tiny triangles in many
different fabrics from the turn of the 20th
century make a perfectly square quilt.
The border and backing are all marks of
an accomplished adult seamstress who
took extra care to make this a quilt with
lasting beauty.

Many doll quilts are designed as
miniature adult-size quilts. Some are
actually too small to cover the larger
dolls of the 19th century. The Whole
Cloth quilt (see Plate 4 and page 29) and
the Bars quilt (see Plate 3 and page 30)
were designed for a miniature doll bed.
Both quilts have cut-out corners that
allow the quilts to wrap easily around

Plate 6

the bed posts. The center of the Whole Cloth quilt was quilted to the dimensions of a specific bed. These quilts were made for display only, not necessarily to comfort a doll.

Another source of doll quilts was unfinished quilt projects and scrap bags of leftover quilt blocks. Some might have been cut from a larger quilt that was damaged or stained. Others simply might have been made from a trial quilt block that never made it into a quilt. One such example is the green and red Carolina Lily quilt (see Plate 6 and page 33) with its interesting and rare example of appliqué work on a doll quilt.

Beginning in the 1880s and continuing well into the 20th century, women's magazines began to offer children's quilts

Pioneer Nebraskan and legendary quiltmaker Grace Snyder writes about burying her stillborn baby girl in her book, *No Time On My Hands*:

A Crazy quilt with featherstitching (see page 67).

"Bert made a coffin from a stout little ammunition box, and I told kind old Grandma Houck where to look in my box cupboard for a lovely little featherstitched doll quilt that Aunt Holly had given me. They wrapped the baby in the little quilt and laid her in the box. Bert buried the coffin at the foot of a little cottonwood tree."[6]

When Grace was able, she went out and put a frame of narrow boards around the little grave.

embroidered with animals and nursery rhymes—images that would appeal to children. These images were offered as transfer patterns for redwork embroidery (see Plate 7 and page 119). Later in the 1920s and 1930s, embroidery patterns for children's clothes and bedding became popular, with Mother Goose nursery-rhyme characters, Beatrix Potter's farm animals, and even Japanese and Dutch children making appearances on doll and crib quilts.

These are not replicas of adult quilts. Their pictorial images appealed to children who recognized them from storybooks read to them at bedtime. The embroidery, too, was too difficult for a child to do. These were definitely made by adults for a child to cherish.

Collecting Doll Quilts

Crib and doll quilts are highly desirable to collectors today. Mary attributes this interest to their manageable size, making them easy to hang, display, and store. They are usually not as expensive as full-size quilts, although the prices have risen sharply in recent years.

A genuine antique doll quilt that is well-made, in good condition, and has documentation is very scarce and expensive. Collectors look for doll quilts that were created as such, rather than simply cut from a larger full-size quilt for sale as a doll quilt. A few tips can help discerning buyers: The quilt design should be proportional to the reduced size of a doll

Plate 7

Plate 8

quilt, the pattern should not appear to be cut off, and the backing and binding should be the same age as the top fabrics. If the doll quilt has a border in the same fabrics as the top, it was probably originally made as a doll quilt.

The Diamonds quilt (see Plate 8 on the facing page and page 34) is prized for the fabrics it contains, but it's not clear whether it was originally made as a doll quilt or cut from a quilt top made for a large bed. The diamonds are not exactly in proportion to a doll-size quilt. The fabrics in the top date from the mid-1800s, but the backing and border fabrics date to the 1880s or even 1900s. The quilt is also machine-quilted, suggesting it was quilted much later than the piecing of the center diamonds. (The sewing machine became a common fixture in middle-class homes in the 1870s, so machine-quilting is sometimes seen in 19th-century quilts.) Speculation aside, Mary decided the fabrics in this quilt were reason enough to purchase it for her collection.

One of Mary's favorite quilts, and one that was obviously made as a doll quilt, is the blue and white Mill Wheel quilt (see Plate 9). Because of its curved piecing, complicated pattern, and precise hand-quilting, she's sure an adult made the quilt for a young child.

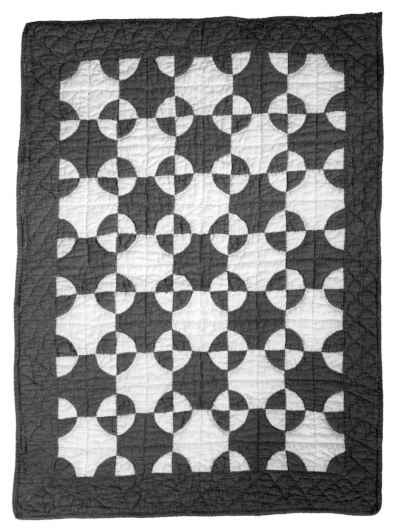

Plate 9 — Mill Wheel, MG 227
Maker unknown. Circa 1930 • 28″ x 21″ • Hand-pieced and hand-quilted.

Mary remembers buying this well-made quilt in 1974 near Winona, Illinois. The quilt was in good condition and priced at $7.50.

Each doll quilt has its own special charm and meaning, whether beautifully made, hurriedly assembled, or showing the clumsy workmanship of a beginner. Busy mothers and grandmothers used leftover blocks, strips, and fabric scraps to hastily make a doll quilt. To speed up the process, they often sewed them by machine or tied them. Some are neither tied nor quilted, but simply lined.

Plate 10

Doll Quilts and Their Stories

One can almost imagine the scene: A young child playing house runs to her mother or grandmother to ask for a cover for her doll. Mother pulls out her box of scraps and makes something quickly. Square-in-a-Square (see Plate 10 and page 93) was possibly made under such circumstances. It contains quilt-block pieces made of fabric scraps, and was quilted by machine with widely-spaced horizontal lines. All in all it makes a delightful quilt for a doll.

The Expanding One-Patch (see Plate 11 and page 105) shows evidence of a child's awkward stitching or a mother's hurried work—with irregular quilting lines

Plate 11

that follow the seams, and machine-stitching by the parent along the outer edge.

Rarely do doll quilts carry the names of the mothers, the children, or the dolls, but when they do they are precious finds. Sometimes the information can help historians find photographs of the quiltmaker and other details about her living situation. All of this information is important to understanding the quilts in their context.

Jan Stehlik, a Nebraska quilt historian and friend of Mary, gave Mary a doll quilt with a pillow that she had acquired at an estate sale in Crete, Nebraska (see Plate 12 and page 127). With the quilt came a note that the girl who made the quilt had died at the age of 12. Jan jotted down the estate owners' names—Olga and Louis Mulonek—and gave this information to Mary.

The unusual family name and the town where they lived made finding information about the family and this young quiltmaker quite simple. Quilt researcher and genealogist Wilene Smith found the family listed as "Malonek" in the 1930 U.S. census. Louis Mulonek (age 30, born in Czechoslovakia) and his wife, Olga F. (age 26, born in Nebraska), had one child named Doris (age 1 year and 8 months, born in Nebraska). Louis and Olga were married about four years when the census was taken.

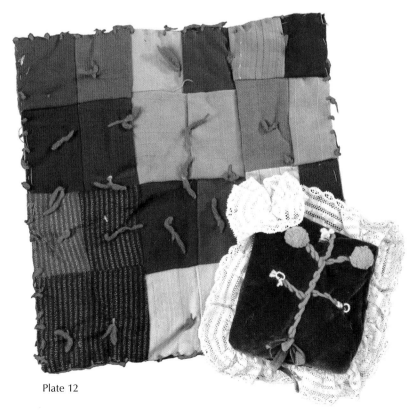

Plate 12

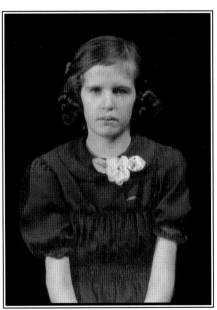

Doris Mulonek
Mary Ghormley Collection

With this information, we know the doll quilt and pillow were made no later than 1940, the year Doris Mulonek died. If Doris made the quilt when she was 5 or 6, it would have been made in the mid-1930s. The doll quilt and pillow suddenly became even more precious to Mary when she learned these new details.

This story underscores the importance of documenting quilts. Information such as a name, date, place a quilt was made, and its story will help people 100 years from now treasure the quilt even more.

The scribbled note that came with Doris Mulonek's quilt and pillow lasted long enough to help quilt enthusiasts many generations later discover the identity of this young girl. Coincidentally, it also helped date the quilt. Without the photo and census information, I might have dated the quilt 1900 to 1910 based on its style and construction, which resembled embroidered Crazy quilts that were popular at that time. Instead, this information moved the date of the quilt up to the 1930s.

Mary's mother-in-law, Nell Botkin Ghormley, made a One-Patch quilt (see Plate 13 and page 128) for Mary's daughters, Peggy, Phyllis, and Marilyn in 1950. Without this information, the quilt

Plate 13

Nell Botkin Ghormley
Roger Ghormley Collection

would be simply "an example of a well-made quilt with circa 1950s fabrics." (See also page 72 for a Crazy quilt Nell Botkin Ghormley made when she was 16.)

Doll quilts have yet to garner serious study, possibly due to the lack of information about the quiltmakers and the children for which they were made. In Mary's collection of 300 doll quilts, only two have inscribed dates, and only one or two quiltmakers' names are known, other than the Ghormley family quilts.

However, even the most rudimentary doll quilts are repositories of early fabrics which interest quilt and textile historians. Although many of the doll quilts were made in Crazy patchwork style or simple block patterns, some are made from published quilt patterns that help date not only the fabrics, but also the quilt itself.

The subsequent chapters present the doll quilts in eras analyzed by styles, fabrics, and patterns. All the quilts were collected by one person. Normally that might skew the sample, but Mary's eye for quiltmaking and collecting make her doll-quilt collection an extraordinary treasure.

A young girl with her doll, circa 1850s.

Virginia Gunn Collection

Early 19th-Century Quilts
(1830s–1860s)

A young girl with her doll, circa 1850.

Virginia Gunn Collection

If a child in the early 1800s wanted to recreate a bedroom for her china doll, she would have looked to the adults' quilts in her house for inspiration, likely scavenging fabrics from her mother's scrap bag. She probably would have wanted the quilt right away and might have tried her hand at making it.

The quilts selected for this chapter are examples of the types of full-size quilts made in the first decades of the 19th century. The styles include Whole Cloth and White-Work quilts, Bar or Strip quilts, and simple pieced Block quilts.

Fabrics available in this period include floral chintz, ombre print, and roller-printed fabrics. Floral chintz was used for bed curtains and spreads in the early 1800s, usually in urban, upper-class homes. The chintz fabrics were imported from Europe and were quite expensive. Women were known to have saved the fabrics when the bed curtains went out of fashion and recycled them in quilts, especially as wide borders.

Beds of this era owned by wealthier families were high four-poster beds with an attached canopy and bed curtains. In New England, quilts were fashioned with two corner sections cut out so that the quilt fit around the bed posts. Two quilts in this collection are exact replicas

Quilt patterns in this period before the Civil War were often based on geometric designs found in tile floors, parquetry, and mosaics. Woven coverlets were another source of inspiration for quilt designs, but prior to 1860 very few quilt patterns had names other than a descriptive term. The early pieced quilt patterns were based on One-Patch, Four-Patch, and Nine-Patch formats.

Stars were popular and were as simple to make with fabrics as with ceramic tiles. The Evening Star (see page 18), with a large square at its center, was another easy pattern to make. The more complicated stars were composed of diamonds that intersected at the center. The bigger the star, the more diamonds were needed for each point.

of adult-size quilts with corners cut out (see Whole Cloth with Fringe on page 29, and Bars, above and on page 30). I suspect they were made by adults.

A word about dating these quilts

None of the doll quilts in this section has a provenance directly related to the children for which they were made. Therefore, we don't know exactly when the quilts were made. It's very likely that some were made to depict an earlier era in which a doll or dollhouse was fashioned. As quilt historians, we learn to work with the material clues in the quilt itself. We compare fabrics to dated textile documents and dated quilts. We know when styles, patterns, and techniques were introduced and when they enjoyed a revival. And then we make our best estimate, conceding that sometimes these material clues may yield an incorrect date.

A young girl with her doll, circa 1850.

Virginia Gunn Collection

Because they have machine-stitching, they probably were not made in the early 19th century, but they are included here because their fabrics may date from this time period.

Quilting designs in the first half of the 19th century, as a rule, were more elaborate and dense. Double and triple parallel lines of quilting, as well as dense, cross-hatch quilting in 10 or more stitches per inch, are much more common in quilts of this era. The same is true for doll quilts.

Following is a gallery of quilts from this period.

Unfortunately, the traditional patterns do not help much in dating a quilt. These early blocks became the core of the quilt-pattern compendium. Today, they are as popular with 21st-century quiltmakers as they were with 19th-century quiltmakers.

One very helpful clue to dating a quilt is the evidence of sewing-machine stitching. The sewing machine was invented in the 1840s but was not widely available until the 1870s, following the Civil War, when domestic sewing was encouraged. Of the quilts presented in this chapter, two have machine-stitching on them (see LeMoyne Star at right and on page 32, and Nine-Patch On Point on page 35).

Plate 14 **Four-Patch with Chintz**, MG 401

Maker unknown. Circa 1850 • 17½" x 17" • Cotton. Hand-pieced. No quilting.

The chintz border dating from the 1830s is probably older than the Four-Patch squares in the center. The woven-tape binding around the outside edge places this quilt in the mid-1800s. With a border on only three sides, the quilt is made so that the pieced blocks cover the surface of the bed and the border falls to the sides and the end of the bed.

Plate 15 Hour Glass, MG 414

Maker unknown. Circa 1840-1850 • 15½″ x 15″ • Cotton. Hand-pieced and hand-quilted diagonally.

This is one of the finer quilts in Mary's collection. Everything about it is right. The roller-printed fabrics in red, blue, and light pinks are all from the first half of the 19th century. The intricate piecing and the tiny binding combined with the appropriate fabrics lead me to believe that this doll quilt was made in the 1840s by an adult for a child.

The simple Hour Glass pattern with perfect intersecting points may have been pieced using the English paper-template technique. This method involves cutting out equal numbers of paper templates and slightly larger cloth pieces. Each cloth piece is folded over the paper template and basted down along the edges. Then the quilter uses a tiny overhand stitch to join the pieces at the abutted edges. Eventually, the basting stitches are removed and the paper comes out. This technique produces precise piecing.

Note how the quiltmaker centered the one print motif on white in the alternate triangles, and then alternated those to form a square diamond in the center. The blue sashing and border are constructed in such a way that the blue fabric becomes a background to the floating squares.

Plate 16 **Whole Cloth with Fringe**, MG 506

Maker unknown. Date unknown. Made in the early 1800s style. • 20″ x 21″ • Linen. Hand-quilted.

All-white Whole Cloth quilts were typically made in the late 1700s and early 1800s. The open areas required the best quilting designs a young woman could muster. The eight-lobed center-quilted medallion in this quilt might have been styled with a compass and pencil. The quiltmaker used blue thread to highlight her quilting. The very thin batting is probably cotton. The all-linen quilt top and backing have been raveled to form fringing on three sides. Full-size quilts of this sort often included quilted dates, initials, or even full names. Unfortunately, this one does not.

Plate 17 **Bars**, MG 433

Maker unknown. Circa 1870 • 17½″ x 17″ • Cotton. Hand-pieced and hand-quilted.

With cut-out corners, this quilt was designed to fit around a doll bed's upright posts. This cut-out corner style is found frequently in adult-size quilts made in the Northeast, but not generally throughout the country. This quilt's fabrics include double-pinks and madder-brown prints, all available in the 1860s and 1870s. The quilt is made completely by hand, most likely by an adult for a doll's bed.

Plate 18 **Evening Star**, MG 526

Maker unknown. Circa 1840 • 18¼″ x 12½″ • Cotton. Hand-pieced and hand-quilted.

This pattern—known as Variable Star, Evening Star, or Ohio Star—is one of the earliest known pieced block patterns dating to the early 1800s. This quilt is full of fabulous early 19th-century printed cottons. The border fabric is a roller-printed cotton, designed in such a way that the layering (or rolling on) of the colors need not be precise. Notice the open beige areas; this fabric is known as an ombre print.

Mary thinks this quilt might have been made by a child. The backing has been brought to the front, turned under, and stitched down unevenly. The hand-quilting is irregular and the lines are not straight.

Plate 19 **LeMoyne Star**, MG 390

Maker unknown • 24″ x 18½″ • Cotton. Hand-pieced. Machine-quilted in diamonds.

This simple eight-point star block is scaled to a doll-size quilt. The layout is arranged so that a single star block is the center block on both the top and bottom rows. (Compare this layout to Plate 18, Evening Star.) Here the inner border is a paisley print in teal green, the backing is a small pink and green print, and the quilt is bound in a green bias binding.

This quilt's date is uncertain. The fabrics clearly date to the 1840s, but the bias tape—introduced in the 20th century—as well as the machine-quilting, suggest it was made in a later era.

Plate 20 **Carolina Lily**, MG 458

Maker unknown. Circa 1850 • 16″ x 12½″
Cotton. Pieced and appliquéd by hand. Hand-quilted.

Detail of
Carolina Lily backing

    This 10-inch Carolina Lily block, which serves as the centerpiece of this doll quilt, was probably salvaged from another quilt project. The work is all hand-done, evidence that an accomplished adult made the quilt. The quilt back, made of an early and very valuable roller-printed chintz fabric dating to the 1850s, is also evidence that this quiltmaker cared deeply for the recipient of this quilt.

    Chintz furnishing fabric, imported from England and France, was a precious commodity. Any chintz scraps left over from making bedroom curtains or bedspreads were saved for handiwork projects such as quilts, pillows, and chair backs.

Plate 21 **Diamonds**, MG 486

Maker unknown. Circa 1870 • 18½" x 18½" • Cotton. Hand-pieced. Machine-quilted.

    This quilt contains many mid-19th-century cotton fabrics. It is machine-quilted in rectangles. The backing is cotton printed with a modernistic blue flower. The wide border is the same fabric as the backing. It's difficult to determine whether this machine-quilted quilt was made as a doll quilt or when it was backed and bound, since the backing fabric appears to be later than the fabric used in the diamonds.

Plate 22 **Nine-Patch on Point**, MG 453

Maker unknown. Circa 1870 • 15½" x 14½" • Cotton. Hand-pieced. Machine-quilted in parallel lines.

The brown fabrics in the center block may be early 19th-century prints. (See similar fabrics in Plate 23, One-Patch.) The flying geese pieced border is made of double-pink print triangles and some purple prints that have faded to light brown. The quilt is bound with a pink print fabric. Most importantly, the quilt is machine-quilted with horizontal parallel lines, which probably indicate a post-1870 date.

Plate 23 **One-Patch**, MG 412

Maker unknown. Circa 1850 • 25½" x 15" • Cotton. Hand-pieced and hand-quilted.

The floral print with a brown background is similar to the brown fabrics in the center block of Plate 22, Nine-Patch on Point. Although it's not possible to date this floral fabric precisely, it was at least designed to convey the look of early 19th-century chintz fabrics. The remaining print fabrics were manufactured in the 1880s, but were designed to resemble cloth of an earlier era.

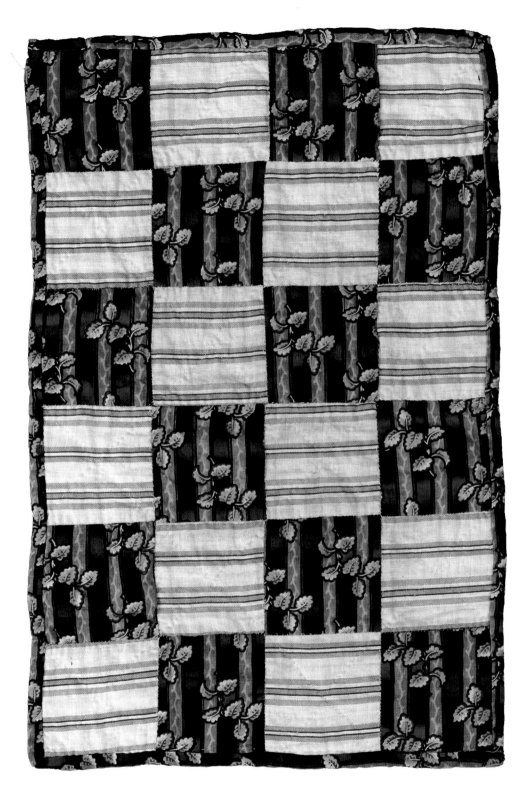

Plate 24 **One-Patch**, MG 525

Maker unknown. Circa 1830s • 14½″ x 10″ • Cotton. Hand-pieced and hand-quilted.

The blue and gold fabric dates from the 1830s. The same fabric is used for the binding.

Plate 25 **Nine-Patch**, MG 437

Maker unknown. Possibly made in Pennsylvania. Circa 1860 • 8″ x 7½″
Cotton. Hand-pieced and hand-quilted.

A child probably made this simple Nine-Patch quilt for her doll. Mary purchased the quilt from an East Coast dealer who said the quilt came from Pennsylvania. It came to Mary as a very worn and dirty textile. Mary decided to wash it. It's one of her favorite pieces.

Plate 26 **Pinwheel or Broken Dishes**, MG 313

Maker unknown. Circa 1850 • 13½" x 9½" • Cotton. Hand-pieced and hand-quilted.

    A doll collector in Connecticut owned this quilt. Mary purchased it with four other doll quilts from a quilt dealer in New York. The quilt dealer thought that it was likely handmade by a child, since the pattern is simple to construct using pieces that are large enough for a child to handle. But no one knows for sure.

Photography by Keethler and Davie
Studio, Columbus, Ohio,
circa 1880s-1890s.

Virginia Gunn Collection

Frontier Quilts
(1870s–1890s)

A young girl, possibly
E. C. Elson, with her doll.
Photo by Elliott's Studio,
Trilla, Illinois.

Virginia Gunn Collection

*F*rontier. The word conjures up images of families in covered wagons moving on to better opportunities, taking with them only the basic necessities in tools, kitchenware, clothing, and bedding.

When these pioneers arrived at their destinations, their high expectations often gave way to the realities of isolation, wind and dirt, rain and mud. *Frontier* conveys resourcefulness, persistence, and patience—making the most of the situation and the resources at hand. And quilts are the embodiment of that frontier spirit. When they were no longer suitable for bedcovers or for recovering with a new top, they were put to other uses: padding for seat cushions, tops for bedsprings, stuffing for insulation, or coverings for farm implements.

Growing up in St. Louis, Missouri, I thought the frontier was the Great Plains far beyond my state's borders. Laura Ingalls Wilder's *Little House on the Prairie* encouraged my flights of imagination. My siblings and I built pioneer houses in the woods behind our house. We cleared the leaves and sticks among the taller trees and constructed make-believe bedrooms, kitchens, and living rooms.

To settlers in Pennsylvania, the frontier was Ohio, Indiana, and Illinois. The same German and Scots-Irish families in Pennsylvania also migrated to the Southeast into the Appalachian Mountains' coves and hollers that reminded them of home. They lived simply, in log cabins with central stone fireplaces. They cleared stones from their steeply sloped land and piled them up to fence in their cows and line their gardens and orchards.

At the heart of frontier survival are mothers and their children. Their lives would make fascinating stories, but few left written accounts. One rare exception is a collection of letters from a Blair family in Bentonville, Arkansas. Six-year-old Maggie wrote on January 25, 1885 to her grandpa in Tennessee:

> I am piecing me a quilt, I have 12 stars done, nearly all of the pieces are scraps that the neighbor girls have give to me, so just please send me a piece of one of your shirts and my aunties' a piece of their dresses to put in my quilt and I will send you a piece of my new dress.[7]

Five years later on July 20, 1890, Maggie's mother wrote to Maggie's aunt, Susan Blair in Tennessee, about Maggie, then 11 years old:

> I have up a quilt now that Maggie pieced. Have quilted two already and have four more to quilt this fall. They are comforts. Susan I must tell you that Maggie is just the nicest and fastest quilter you ever saw for her age.

It would surprise you to see how much she will get done and that well done too in an afternoon.[8]

The doll quilts selected for this chapter were probably made from the 1870s through the 1890s, except for the Log Cabin quilts, which date to circa 1900. Log Cabin quilts are featured here because they evoke the essence of the frontier experience—the hearth at the center of each block surrounded by logs. Made of leftover scraps, the Log Cabin quilts, because of their layered construction, make warm, heavy comforters. The fun of making a Log Cabin quilt was watching the pattern emerge as the blocks were joined together. A leftover block, or one that just didn't fit in a full-size quilt, made a quick doll-size quilt.

Also featured in this chapter are classic pieced patterns (Four-Patch, Nine-Patch, and Sawtooth Star) made of printed fabrics in madder browns and oranges that were available during this time period. This era witnessed a veritable calico explosion. The production of printed textiles in the United States in 1880 reached 800 million yards annually. Assuming only half of the United States population of 60 million were wearing print dresses, American textile companies produced enough printed fabric for each woman to have 17 dresses with appropriate trimmings and flounces.[9]

Fabric was transported in various ways—by train, riverboat, and rural free postal delivery. Dry-goods stores appeared at rural crossroads. Peddlers in wagons traveled from farm to farm on a regular basis to sell or trade products that farm wives needed. In areas where cotton was grown, local cotton mills sold thread and cloth, spun or woven from cotton grown on nearby farms. A trip to the store or mill to buy household necessities also gave an opportunity to buy some calico and visit with friends.

By the late 19th century, the price of sewing machines fell to an affordable range for middle-class women. This, combined with the availability of calico and the need for bedding for growing families, created a healthy resurgence of home-sewing and quiltmaking, even in isolated farming communities.

Where were the children in this picture? With their natural curiosity and desire to be in the middle of things, children must have been tugging at their mothers' sewing, climbing into their laps, or working the treadles on those new-fangled sewing machines. One can easily imagine mothers cutting out scraps for inquisitive children to amuse and entertain themselves by making doll quilts.

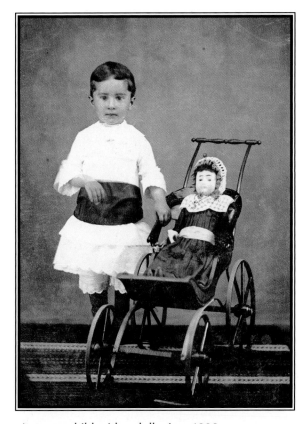

A young child with a doll, circa 1880s.

Virginia Gunn Collection

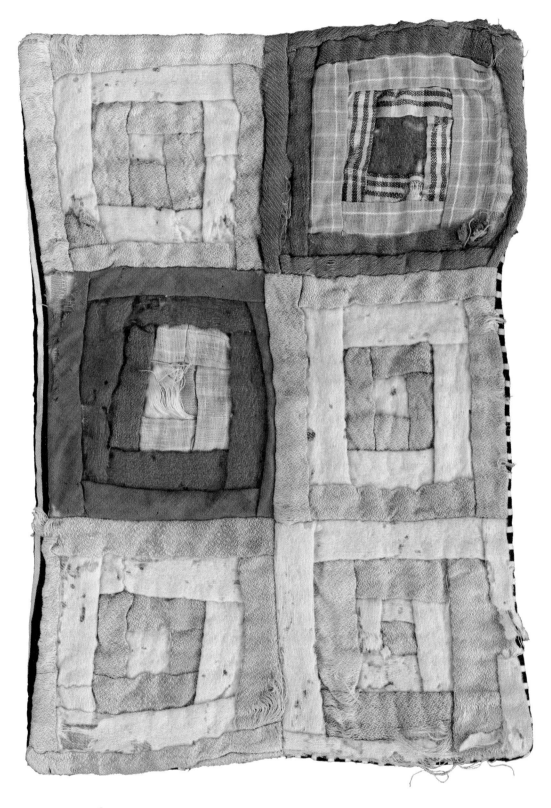

Plate 27 Log Cabin, MG 226

Maker unknown. Circa 1880 • 12" x 8" • Wool challis, cottons. Hand-pieced. Not quilted.

Mary is almost certain that this quilt is child-made: "The quilt has different-sized squares. Only one square has a red center and it is bigger than the others. The sides are not straight. It has personality—I like it."

Plate 28 Log Cabin, MG 491

Maker unknown. Circa 1900 • 18″ x 12½″ • Cotton. Hand-pieced and hand-quilted.

The block, with one large square in the center and log strips added to form concentric borders, is often called Housetop. Narrow strips of four-block patches have been added at the top and bottom. This style is commonly used among the African-American quilting group in Gee's Bend, Alabama, whose full-size quilts have been featured in exhibits around the country.

Plate 29 Log Cabin, MG 332

Maker unknown. Circa 1900-1910 • 21″ x 18½″ • Cotton. Hand-pieced and hand-quilted.

The placement of contrasting fabrics creates a completely different overall effect than that of Plate 28, Log Cabin. This quilt has no batting. In fact, the quilt's backing is the foundation cloth used to piece the Log Cabin block. The front fabrics are turned to the back to form a binding.

Plate 30 **Log Cabin – Sunshine and Shadow,** MG 223

Maker unknown. Circa 1890 • 22″ x 15″ • Cotton. Hand-pieced and hand-quilted.

The various arrangements of Log Cabin blocks create dazzling quilts. Here the blocks are constructed with light and dark log strips added alternately, which create a diagonal cutting across the block. Arranging the log strips in certain ways creates overall patterns with names that, surprisingly, have remained consistent over the generations. This one is called Sunshine and Shadow.

Plate 31 Log Cabin – Sunshine and Shadow, MG 333

Maker unknown. Circa 1900 • 12¾″ x 10″ • Cotton. Hand-pieced. Tied.

With slightly larger strips and not precisely pieced, this quilt was probably made by a child. It is tied with yellow yarn. The backing is a striped cotton flannel.

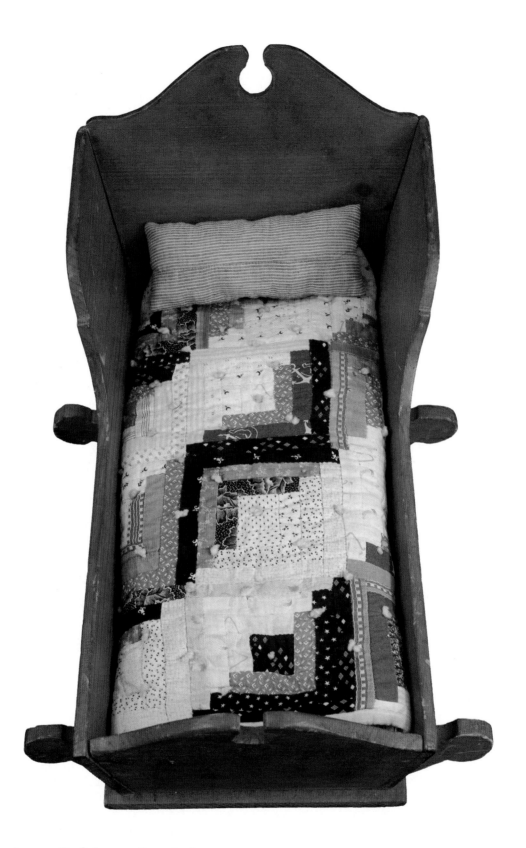

Plate 32 **Log Cabin – Straight Furrow**, MG 496

Maker unknown. Circa 1900 • 17¼″ x 13¾″ • Cotton. Hand-pieced. Tied.

This arrangement is called Straight Furrow. The dark and light rays formed by the smaller logs create strong diagonals across the quilt's surface.

Detail of
Sixteen-Patch backing

Plate 33 **Sixteen-Patch**, MG 205

Maker unknown. Circa 1880s • 12½″ x 9½″ • Cotton. Hand-pieced. Not quilted.

The fabrics of the quilt top include a double-pink print, a woven-brown check, and a double-green print. The binding is a paisley fabric which also appears on the lining of the quilt.

Mary: "I think this quilt is child-made. The stitching is very crude. Notice how three corners are rounded, but not the fourth. Even without any quilting, it has a certain charm to it."

Plate 34 **Hit-or-Miss**, MG 383

Maker unknown. Circa 1880s • 13″ x 10″ • Cotton. Hand-pieced. Not quilted.

The fabrics in this doll quilt are very likely from the Cocheco Printworks of Dover, New Hampshire. In the 1880s, the company printed fabrics in paisley and florals on brown backgrounds (seen here and in Plate 33, Sixteen-Patch). Mary named this quilt Hit-or-Miss because it lacks a particular pattern. It was likely made from salesman fabric samples.

Plate 35 **Four-Patch**, MG 512

Maker unknown. Circa 1860s-80s • 10″ x 9½″ • Cotton. Hand-pieced. Not quilted.

The cotton printed fabrics in this quilt have the brown, rust, and light-beige colorations of fabrics popular from the 1860s through the 1880s. Double-green patches are evident in the quilt top. A double-pink print fabric is used as the binding. (Double-green and double-pink print fabrics point to the 1860s date.)

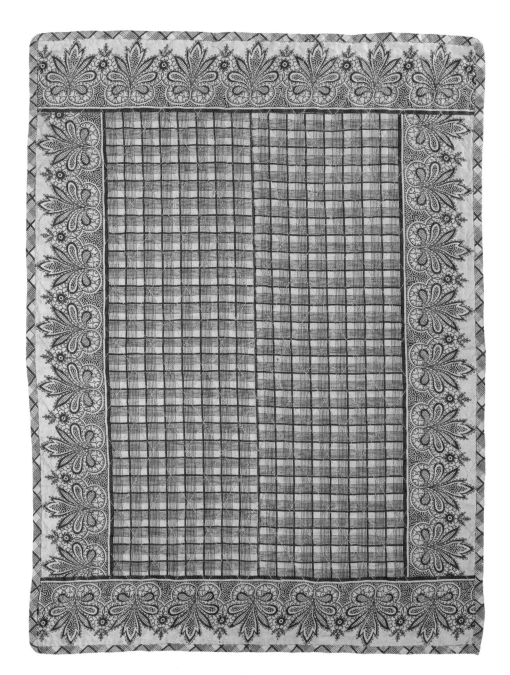

Detail of Whole Cloth backing showing machine-quilting

Plate 36 **Whole Cloth**, MG 466

Maker unknown. Circa 1870s-80s • 19½" x 14½" • Cotton. Machine-quilted.

Cocheco Printworks of Dover, New Hampshire, produced fabric in these colors and with printed lace along one selvage of the cloth. Printed lace is often seen in Log Cabin quilts and Crazy quilts. The two halves in the center of this quilt are seamed along the center line. The lace edging at the left and right are not seamed. The fabric was printed this way. The lace edgings at the top and bottom have been cut from the bolt and seamed to the center panel as border fabric.

The backing of this quilt has two interesting features. The fabric is a dark-brown stripe, popular in the 1870s and 1880s. Also impressive are the precisely cross-hatched quilting lines which are machine-stitched using a chain stitch. Such stitching would have been common for jacket linings. It's highly likely that this quilt was made by a professional tailor or seamstress.

Plate 37 **Four-Patch**, MG 327

Maker unknown. Circa 1870s-80s • 20″ x 13½″ • Cotton top. Wool back. Tied.

Mary: "I decided I had to have this quilt even though it likely was cut from an adult-size quilt, since the blocks were not scaled down. That practice usually spoils a quilt for me, but I bought this one for the fabrics it contains—double-green prints from the 1850s and a white wool blanket for the backing."

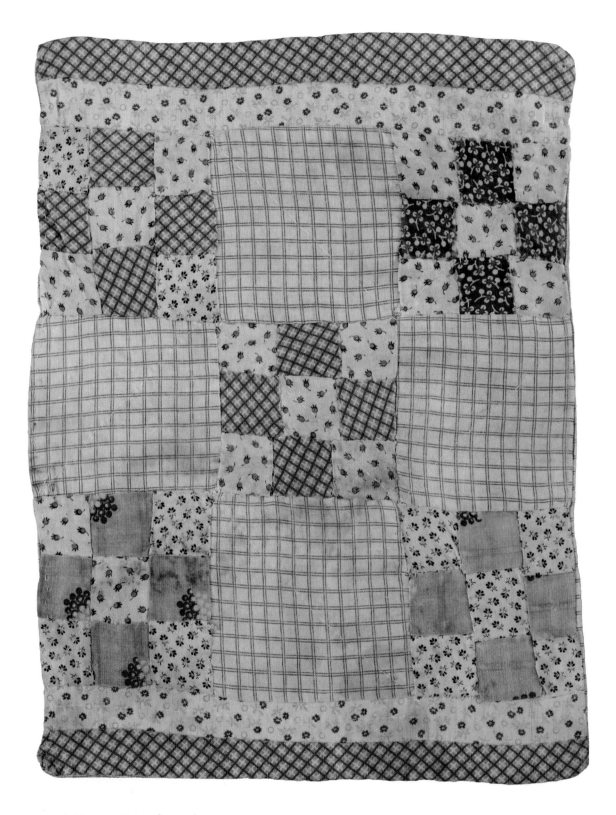

Plate 38 **Nine-Patch**, MG 235

Maker unknown. Circa 1880s-90s • 11½" x 8½" • Cotton. Hand-pieced and hand-quilted diagonally.

The Nine-Patch pattern has a long history dating back to the mid-19th century. Mary purchased this quilt in 1990. The antique dealer told her it was from an estate in Broken Bow, Nebraska, and that the family homesteaded from Indiana to Nebraska in the 1870s.

Plate 39 **Sawtooth Star**, MG 273

Maker unknown. Circa 1870s-80s • 17″ x 14″
Cotton. Hand-pieced and hand-quilted.

Mary: "I really like this quilt for its miniature patterns and the skill required to make those stars. For this reason, I believe it's not child-made. I also like the two borders. The back is mended and has many stains, but this only adds to the charm. The back also shows some kind of trademark. This quilt was clearly made using fabrics someone had on hand."

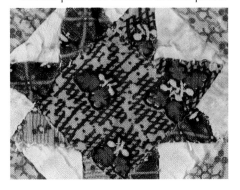

Children with a wool embroidered
Crazy quilt, 1880s-1910s.

Merikay Waldvogel Collection

Victorian Crazy Quilts

(1880s–1910s)

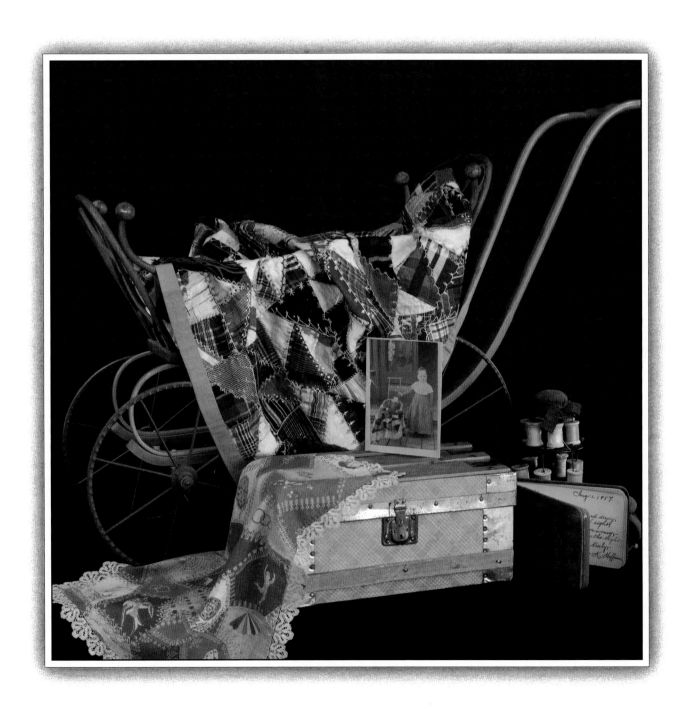

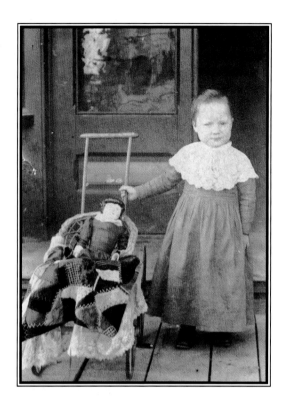

A girl with her doll and a Crazy quilt with a lace border, circa 1900.

Virginia Gunn Collection

Crazy quilts—once scorned as crude, garish, and ostentatious— today attract collectors and researchers for various reasons. They are repositories of thousands of pieces of cloth and an infinite variety of embroidered images. The intended goal of Crazy quilts was to display the finest, most effete fabrics one could. Quiltmakers went to all ends to acquire these fabrics—ordering salesmen sample books, trading scraps with fellow quilters far away through letter-writing, gathering up scraps from a seamstress's work table, buying bundles of scraps from dress factories, and cutting up boyfriends' neckties.

The embroidery was supposed to be varied and elaborate. Embellishments such as ribbon embroidery and beading were encouraged. Painting on velvet and taffeta pieces was considered a shortcut but also a required skill. Those who excelled created textile treasures. Certain embroidered or painted images recur frequently in Crazy quilts because instruction booklets offered transfer patterns and directions for making the embellishments. These common images include spider webs, interlocking circles, stars, owls, flowers, and children at play. Photographic transfers also found their place in Crazy quilts, and many Crazy quilts have embroidered names and dates on them.

Crazy quilts, depending on where they were made and who made them, contained silks, velvets, and taffetas as well as cotton prints and even wool. The silk and velvet varieties trimmed in lace are often associated with middle- and upper-middle-class families living in urban areas. The decorating tastes at the time were eclectic, even hodge-podge. As is evident in this photo of a family in their front parlor, nearly every surface was covered with knick-knacks, textiles, ceramics, and sculptures.

Doll quilts made in the Crazy-quilt style are often made of cotton fabrics and

A family photo in a parlor, circa 1900. Photo by A. W. Harrison, Selma, Alabama. *Merikay Waldvogel Collection.*

do not have much embroidery associated with the silk and velvet Crazies. This may be due to their intended use and the need for frequent laundering.

This advertising trade card is illustrated on one side with a Crazy quilt and on the other side with "100 Crazy Patchwork Stitches." Each side has an open area for the business name and address, in this case a shoe store in Akron, Ohio. Why would a shoe store hand out advertising or trade cards with embroidery stitches on it? To attract the women and girls who were caught up in the frenzy of making Crazy quilts. Not only were the cards colorful and instructional, they were also collectible, thus increasing their advertising potential.

Trade Card: "Compliments of E. W. Brinkman's Fine Shoes, Akron, Ohio" *Merikay Waldvogel Collection*

Plate 40 **Crazy**, MG 192

Maker unknown. Circa 1885 • 14″ x 14″ • Cotton. Hand-sewn. Not quilted.

The front of this quilt is a veritable kaleidoscope of 1880s cotton dress fabrics, many of which probably came from Cocheco Printworks in Dover, New Hampshire. Note especially the medium browns with small floral prints and the paisley prints.

The backing fabric, on the facing page, with scenes from Charles Dickens' *Pickwick Papers* is definitely linked to Cocheco Printworks. Diane Fagan Affleck confirmed that the American Textile History Museum owns a ledger book kept by a finisher employed at Cocheco. The book is labeled January to April 1880. The Pickwick print is dated April 20, 1880.[10]

Plate 41 **Backing of Crazy**, MG 192

According to textile historian Deborah Kraak, 19th-century fabric printed in patchwork was very popular in the 1880s. It was referred to as "patchwork style," "patches," and "patchwork robe" in textile company correspondence. The word "robe" indicated a type of fabric with large-scale print suitable for dressing gowns.[11] It is interesting to note that printed patchwork is perfectly suited to doll quilts—no sewing or quilting is required.

Plate 42 Crazy with Lace, MG 445

Maker unknown. Circa 1890 • 18″ x 14″ • Cotton. Not quilted.

Detail of
Crazy with Lace

This faux Crazy quilt has both top and backing fabrics preprinted in a Crazy-quilt design, complete with elaborately embroidered faux edging stitches, butterflies, owls, spiders, and children playing. Even a faux embroidered "Mother" is partially visible along the bottom edge. This quilt has no batting or quilting stitches. The lace edging is machine-stitched to all four sides of the doll quilt.

According to Diane Fagan Affleck of the American Textile History Museum in Lowell, Massachusetts, this fabric was probably manufactured by Merrimack Printworks in the 1880s, although she could not verify the date of manufacture. The museum contains company records, but she found no printing record for this Crazy-quilt print.

Plate 43 Crazy with Hour Glass, MG 187

Maker unknown. Circa 1890 • 18″ x 15″ • Cotton. Hand-sewn. Not quilted.

This oddly-shaped piece without any quilting was probably made by a young child for her doll's cradle. At the top edge are two Hour Glass blocks which may have been the child's own attempt at piecing quilt blocks. The madder prints, shirting prints, mourning prints, and red and white prints (see Glossary) are all typical dress fabrics of the 1880s–90s period.

Plate 44 **Crazy**, MG 189

Maker unknown. Circa 1900 • 15″ x 10″ • Cotton. Hand-sewn and hand-quilted.

The medium-blue, navy-blue, and maroon prints have supplanted the brown fabrics in this doll quilt and reflect the change in colors of dress fabrics during this period. Red with polka-dots and the black mourning prints remain. Note also the woven navy and white checked fabric which became popular for women's dresses at the turn of the 20th century.

One can imagine this quilt also being made by a child, but unlike Plate 43, Crazy with Hour Glass, this piece is simply quilted. One line of quilting uses black thread, which may have been the child's attempt at hand-quilting. The rest of the quilting is with white thread.

Plate 45 Crazy, MG 190

Maker unknown. Circa 1900 • 16″ x 16″
Cotton. Hand sewn. Not quilted.

Detail of Crazy, MG 190

Mary: "This quilt is probably adult-made, the charming fabric shapes probably leftover pieces from a sewing project. The fabrics lie flat and are edged with simple embroidery stitches.

"The muslin foundation cloth is visible in places, and the separate binding is a solid red cloth. The bright red and white prints, a woven plaid, and shirting prints all suggest a date of 1890s-1910s."

Plate 46 **Crazy**, MG 315

Maker unknown. Circa 1900 • 18½″ x 13″ • Tie silk. Hand-sewn. Not quilted or tied.

This striking quilt was made from men's ties. Both sides of the quilt are worked in the Crazy-quilt style (see backing on facing page). Notice even the binding is made of various pieces. This is no doubt a quilt made by an adult for a child's doll.

Plate 47 Backing of Crazy, MG 315

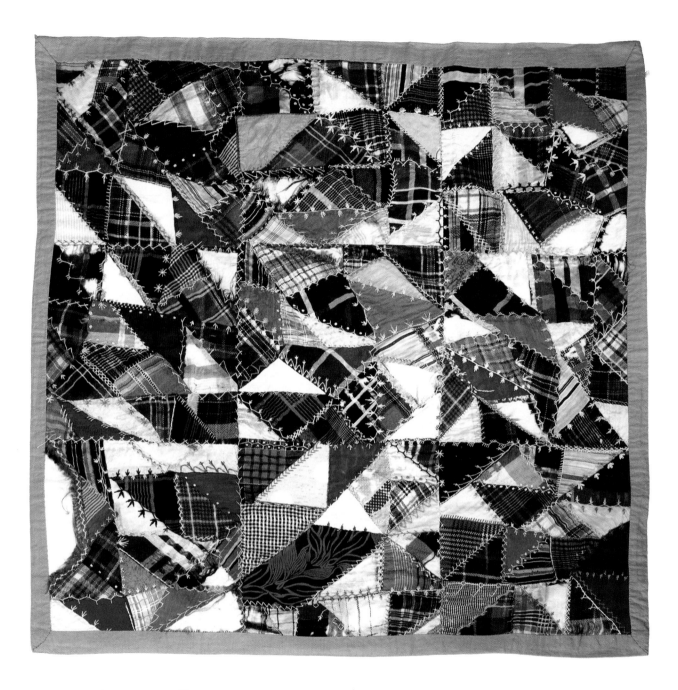

Plate 48 Crazy, Silk, MG 194

Maker unknown. Circa 1900 • 28" x 28" • Crepe, rayon, silk, and velvet. Hand sewn. Not quilted or tied.

This doll quilt—with oddly-shaped pieces of silk, rayon, velvet, crepe, and lots of embroidery—is more typical of the classic Crazy quilts. It also includes printed velvets and woven rayon-plaid ribbons. The fuchsia-pink backing has been folded over to the front to form a binding on four sides.

A wide variety of embroidery stitches outlines the shapes. The era's growing interest in Crazy quilts not only fed an interest in acquiring many samples of fabrics, but also increased demand for Crazy-quilt stitching patterns. This particular quilt is covered with different types of stitching. Because the stitches are not perfectly rendered, the quilt was likely made by a young girl for use as a doll quilt or as an accessory to her bedroom furnishings.

Plate 49 Crazy, MG 316

Maker unknown. Circa 1900 • 10½″ x 5½″ • Cotton. Hand-pieced. Not quilted.

Mary: "This was surely made by a child for a doll. It's a little odd, but very charming. It looks like the child attempted to piece a block with tiny pieces and then moved on to larger pieces. The backing is white muslin. There is no batting and no quilting. It is sewn entirely by hand."

Plate 50 Crazy, MG 191

Made by Nell Maria Botkin Ghormley (1888-1956). Made in 1904 • 16" x 16"
Crepe, rayon, and silk. Not quilted. Machine-stitched along the outside edges.

This Crazy pieced pillow cover is inscribed "Maria 1904." We know a lot about Maria because she was Mary's mother-in-law. She was born on October 15, 1888. In 1904, when she inscribed her name here, she was 16. She married John Raymond Ghormley on October 15, 1913 in Hutchinson, Kansas. Their second child, Roger—Mary's husband—was born November 3, 1918. In later years, she was known as Nell Botkin Ghormley. (See page 128 for a One-Patch quilt she made as an adult for her grandchildren.)

The facing page shows the beginning of of an extended story about a young girl and her efforts to collect fabric to make a Crazy quilt. The story reminds me of Nell Maria Botkin Ghormley, who made her Crazy quilt when she was roughly the same age as the girl in this story.[12]

Nell Maria Botkin
Ghormley, circa 1900.
Roger Ghormley Collection

Golden Days

FOR BOYS AND GIRLS.

[Entered according to Act of Congress, in the year 1887, by James Elverson, in the Office of the Librarian of Congress, at Washington, D. C.]

VOL. VIII. | JAMES ELVERSON, Publisher, N.W. corner NINTH and SPRUCE Sts. | PHILADELPHIA MAY 21, 1887. | TERMS: $3.00 PER ANNUM, IN ADVANCE. | No. 25.

LINDA'S CRAZY QUILT.

BY FANNIE WILLIAMS.

"Oh, dear!" sighed Linda Trafton, turning over the pages of a closely-written, school-girlish letter, which her brother Fred had tossed into her lap, on returning from the post office. "I do wish I could get silk pieces enough to make a crazy quilt. Cousin Dell writes all about hers, and it must be very pretty."

"Crazy quilt! That's about all I've heard for the last six months! I should think you girls had all gone crazy yourselves!" ejaculated Fred.

"Why, Fred!" was Linda's only answer to this outburst.

She was a very sweet-tempered little maid, with soft, brown hair and soft, brown eyes, that matched in color as exactly as eyes and hair could match, and gave her a look of being—as indeed she was—too gentle to dispute, or even to argue, with anybody, least of all with Fred, who was fifteen, and three years her elder, and always took a tone of great superiority toward his little sister.

Still, he was a pretty good sort of brother, as brothers go; and, in Linda's eyes, he was a prodigy of cleverness.

So, whenever they happened to differ in opinion, and Fred expressed himself in this vehement style, she only looked at him in a deprecating way, and murmured:

"Why, Fred!"

"Well, I should like to know," continued Fred, "what could be more idiotic than the way you spend your time, you girls, fitting those ridiculous, catty-cornered pieces of silk together, and working them all over with bugs and cobwebs and caterpillars, and little boys in Mother Hubbard dresses! You may well call 'em *crazy* quilts! I don't believe there was ever anything crazier, unless it was the lunatic who first invented them!"

"Why, Fred!" said Linda, again. "Now, I think they are too pretty for anything!"

"Pretty!" snorted Fred. "They're made out of the last things that you'd suppose anybody would ever think of putting into a bed-quilt. I can't get a chance to wear a neck-tie half out before somebody wants it. Kate Graham spoke for my last new one the next day after I bought it. And I hardly dare to put my hat down, where there's a girl around, for fear she'll capture my hat-band!"

By this time, Linda was laughing outright.

"Oh, you are so funny, Fred! But you only just ought to see Kate Graham's crazy quilt. I *know* you couldn't help calling it lovely. She has got pieces of ever so many wedding dresses in it; but I don't know who would give *me* any. Aunt Mary never will get married, nor Cousin Susie, nor our Bridget, unless Pat hurries up with his courting—and there's nobody else. Besides, they are all making crazy quilts of their own. I would start one with papa's old silk handkerchief and his Association badge, if I thought I could ever get pieces enough to finish it; but I don't see how I could."

"Bess Hartley told me that she was going to send off somewhere and get a lot of pieces that are put up to sell. You get a whole package of assorted colors for a dollar," suggested Fred.

"Oh, that would make it cost too much! Mamma would not let me do that," said Linda, shaking her head. "She says it is well enough to use up odd bits of silk in that way, if one happens to have them; but she doesn't think it right to spend money in such a manner, instead of using it for better purposes—and I don't suppose it is."

"Well, I am sure I don't know what you are going to do," was Fred's consoling observation. "You'd be as crazy as the rest of the girls if you began to piece a quilt; and I don't know but you will go crazy if you can't."

With which conclusion, Fred walked off whistling, and left Linda to read her Cousin Dell's letter over again, and wish that Patrick O'Brien would propose to Bridget, if he was ever going to, so that she could get married, and have a new silk dress for her wedding.

However, Linda was not the girl to fret and worry after things which were unattainable.

Fred would have his joke, but she was not going to make herself unhappy just because she had not the materials for making silk patchwork, as

"OH, MRS. BURBANK! WHAT BEAUTIFUL PIECES!" CRIED LINDA.
"WHERE DID THEY ALL COME FROM?"

Dell and the rest of her girl friends were doing. There were plenty of other pleasures and amusements within her reach, and the one that she enjoyed most of all came in her way, as it happened, the very next morning.

Her father said to her, as he rose from the table after breakfast:

"Linda, would you like a ride, my dear? I am going to drive over to East Berlin, and I will take you along, if you would like to go."

"*If* I would like it! Why, papa, you *know* there isn't *anything* that I like so much as a good, long ride with you!" cried Linda, dancing with delight, as she ran off to get ready for the drive.

For it was indeed a "good long" ride to East Berlin—fifteen miles at least—and

Photography by Bartoo Studio,
Rensselaer, Indiana, circa 1880s-1890s.

Virginia Gunn Collection

Quilt Patterns
(1880s–1910s)

This child is seated on a pieced-pattern quilt top, circa 1904-1918.

Merikay Waldvogel Collection

Following the end of the Civil War in 1865, entrepreneurs turned their attention from the military to the domestic market. Salesmen representing sewing-machine manufacturers and textile mills fanned out across the nation, hawking their goods to store owners in small towns and growing urban cities. Rural free-mail delivery was established, which meant that even the most remote farm families had access through mail-order catalogs and weekly magazines to the latest products and fabrics of the day.

In the 1880s and 1890s, a number of new women's magazines debuted with a stated purpose of providing for the needs and interests of the home and family. In fact, they were vehicles for significant amounts of advertising. The magazines included: *Farm and Home*, *Farm and Fireside*, *Fireside Visitor*, *Good Stories*, *Happy Hours*, *Hearth and Home*, *The Household*, *Ohio Farmer*, and *Ladies Home Companion*. They carried short stories, recipes, gardening tips, decorating ideas, and tips and patterns for knitting, crocheting, tatting, and quiltmaking.

The editors encouraged reader participation and input. *Hearth and Home*'s "Mutual Benefit" column became a place for woman-to-woman interaction. Functioning much like the World Wide

Web and e-mail today, these farm magazines served an important role for sharing information, bartering, and friendship:

Would any of the sisters like to make a calico patchwork quilt for me? I have many pieces but no time or patience to make the quilt.
— *Mrs. J. A. Chadil, Queens, L. I.* [13]

Pieced blocks for calico quilt (necktie), wool quilt (chip-basket), for best offer. Write.
— *Mrs. Anna Wilson, Geddes, S. Dak.* [14]

I would appreciate quilt blocks, 12 x 12 inches "Electric Fan" or "St Valentine" pattern, made of two colors and white—that is, of dark and light calico and cotton. Will return the favor. Please outline name and address in any color.
— *Mrs. C. L. Bork, Hallton, Pa.* [15]

L. E. Lonely. Newtonia, Mo., has a pretty patchwork pattern called "Old Maid's Puzzle," to exchange for pieces of print four inches square. [16]

Mrs. Nellie B. Hoffman, Sidney, N. J., would like a pattern with diagram of patchwork, called "Ocean Wave," in exchange for one called "Peter's Puzzle." [17]

Pattern of "Japanese Lily" quilt block, for same of "Garfield's Monument."
—*Martha J. Case, Randall, Ks.* [18]

Editors sometimes printed quilt-pattern blocks submitted by their readers. The quilt title was printed under the illustration. With wide distribution throughout the country, this naming of blocks led to a standardization of patterns and names.

The Ladies Art Company of St. Louis, Missouri, published a catalog of several hundred quilt-block illustrations in 1897.

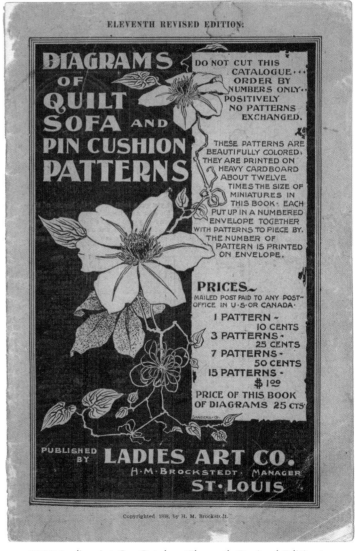

1898 *Ladies Art Co.* Catalog (Eleventh Revised Edition)
Merikay Waldvogel Collection

Many appeared first in farm and home magazines. For 10 cents per pattern, the quilter could order a block by name and number. She received a color card showing the pattern and an envelope of tissue-paper templates for piecing. The 25-cent catalog became a ready source of quilt-pattern names and illustrations for not only quilters, but also for quilt designers and columnists during the quilt revivals of the 1920s and '30s.

Marie Webster, Ruth Finley, and Carrie Hall, who in the early 20th century wrote the first quilt history books, referenced the *Ladies Art Co.* catalog. The Nancy Cabot quilt patterns, published several times a week in the *Chicago Tribune* beginning in 1933, are very close renditions of the *Ladies Art Co.* patterns. Some even carry the same names and design instructions.

The quilts in this chapter reflect the pattern names found in primary sources, such as the late 19th-century farm magazines and the *Ladies Art Co.* catalog. These sources contain some of the earliest occurrences of pattern names assigned to these doll quilts.

A girl in a white-eyelet dress with her doll, circa 1890s.

Virginia Gunn Collection

Plate 51 **Sugar Loaf**, MG 285

Maker unknown. Circa 1890s • 21″ x 16″ • Cotton. Hand-pieced and hand-quilted diagonally.

The pattern name Sugar Loaf refers to the conical-shaped sugar blocks used in Colonial American homes when sugar was a treasured commodity kept under lock and key in a sugar chest. The pattern was featured in the first issue of the *Ladies Art Co.* The earliest reference to the name and pattern configuration was in *Farm and Fireside* magazine published in March 1, 1887.

Mary: "Because the pattern is not scaled down to doll-size, it's possible this quilt was cut from a larger quilt made for a full-size bed. I love the late 1800s fabrics—mourning prints, red and black prints, manganese browns, and navy-blue print fabrics. The tan print in the alternate blocks is printed with morning glories."

Ladies Art Co.

No. 370   Size 10x10
Sugar Loaf.

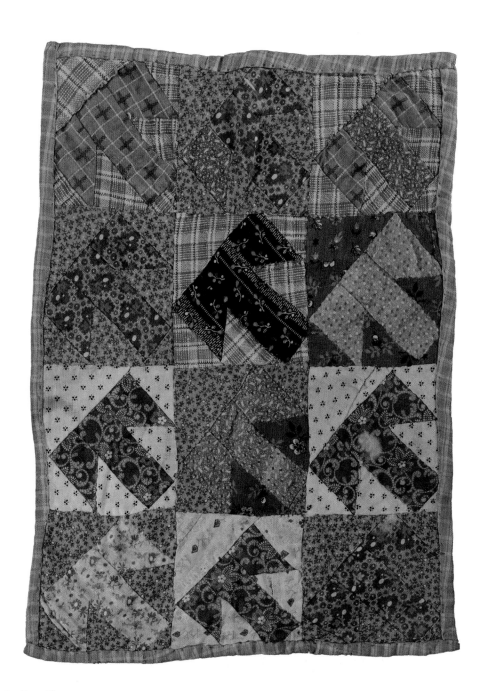

Plate 52 T Quilt, MG 463

Maker unknown. Circa 1880-1890 • 13″ x 10″ • Cotton. Hand-pieced. Machine-quilted.

The double-pink, dark-brown, and red and black printed fabrics were all available in the 1880s and 1890s. The brown and white woven-cotton backing was brought to the front to form a binding. The pattern, known as the Letter T Block, was published in the August 1, 1891 issue of *Farm and Home*. Other quilt designers and magazines published the same pattern in the first half of the 20th century.

Ladies Art Co. renamed the *Farm and Home* pattern and offered it in two formats—one right side up (#86 T Quartet) and the other upside down (#85 Mixed T).

Ladies Art Co.

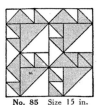

No. 85 Size 15 in.
Mixed T.

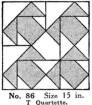

No. 86 Size 15 in.
T Quartette.

Plate 53 **Brown Goose**, MG 314

Maker unknown. Circa 1890 • 16″ x 11″ • Cotton. Hand-pieced and hand-quilted.

The February 15, 1883 *Louisville Farm and Fireside* named this block Double Z, which was carried on by the *Ladies Art Co.* in its 1897 catalog. Other names for the pattern were Scarlet Wave (1906 *Happy Hours*) and Old Maid's Puzzle (1906 *Clara Stone's Quilt Patterns* catalog).

This pattern is sometimes called Gray Goose, depending on the color of the calicos in the quilt. The word "goose" may refer to a goose that provided feathers for the family's bed and pillows. Or it may come from the old lullaby, "The Old Gray Goose is Dead."[19]

Louisville Farm and Fireside 1883
Double Z

Plate 54 Churn Dash, MG 168

Maker unknown. Circa 1900 • 16½″ x 12″ • Cotton. Hand-pieced and hand-quilted.

In the February 15, 1883 issue of *Louisville Farm and Fireside*, a reader identified only as Emma C. of Wyoming, Iowa, sent in four patterns: Capital T, A Wrench, Double Z, and Double X. She wrote: "Many of the quilt patterns you have sent are so pretty, I thought I would add my mite by sending some of mine."

In the *Ladies Art Co.* catalog, published 14 years later in 1897, this pattern was titled Double Wrench. The quilt's estimated date (1900) is based on its cotton fabrics in navy, maroon, gray, red and white checks, as well as shirting fabrics with black figures, including polka-dots. The quilt is lined with a brown and white checked fabric. All these fabrics were available and popular around 1900.

Louisville Farm and Fireside 1883
A Wrench

Plate 55   **Double T Square**, MG 201

Maker unknown. Circa 1890 • 16½″ x 16½″
Cotton. Hand-pieced and hand-quilted.

Capital T also appeared in *Louisville Farm and Fireside* (February 15, 1883). For the doll quilt, the quiltmaker might have used the arrangement of the center diamond and four pieced corners from the *Ladies Art Co.* pattern #144, Mrs. Cleveland's Choice.

Ladies Art Co.

No. 144   Size 15 in.
Mrs. Cleveland's Choice.

*Louisville Farm
and Fireside 1883*
Capital T

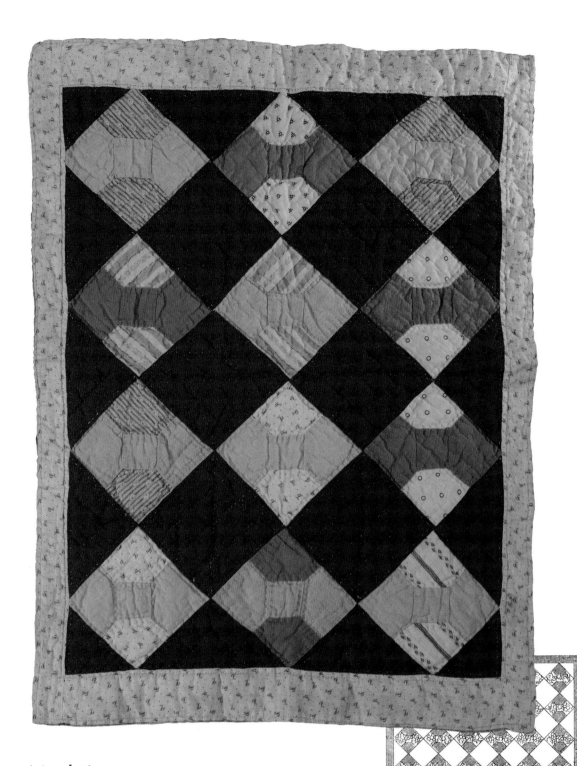

Plate 56 Necktie, MG 401

Maker unknown. Circa 1910 • 21½″ x 15″ • Cotton. Hand-pieced and hand-quilted. Machine stitched along outer border.

The *Ladies Art Co.* catalog offered this pattern in various layouts: #119 Necktie (a single 9-inch block), #262 True Lover's Knot (four blocks without alternating plain blocks), and #145 Joseph's Necktie (five blocks with alternating plain blocks).

Ladies Art Co. #119 Necktie

Detail of Medallion backing

Plate 57 Medallion, MG 404

Maker unknown. Circa 1910 • 22" x 18"
Cotton. Hand-pieced. Machine-quilted.

This reversible quilt contains many fabrics of the early 20th century—including double-pinks, gingham, plaids, and medium-blue fabrics with white prints. One side is a star block made of various scrap fabrics, but the other side is the letter M. Although we don't know the maker's name, I wouldn't be a bit surprised if the child's name began with an M.

The Letter M quilt-block was published in *Hearth and Home* in February 1906. A reader named "Busybody" from Erie, Kansas, submitted it. She suggested that this style of letter makes a charming "initial" or "alphabet" quilt. When using several blocks in one quilt top, the editors advised to "omit the border in every other block, thus making the border do for joining and the quilt entirely of pieced work."

Hearth and Home

"Letter **M**" Quilt-block
This style of letter makes a charming

"LETTER **M**" QUILT-BLOCK

"initial" or "alphabet quilt." Cut the strips for the block two inches wide and omit the border in every other block, thus making the border do for joining and the quilt entirely of pieced work. Busybody. Erie, Kans.

Plate 58 Hour Glass Sawtooth Star, MG 443

Ladies Art Co.

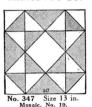

No. 347 Size 13 in.
Mosaic, No. 19.

Maker unknown. Circa 1900 • 15½" x 13½"
Cotton. Hand pieced. Machine-quilted and machine-bound.

The *Ladies Art Co.* catalog carried a series of 22 Mosaic blocks simply labeled Mosaic 1 through 22. The pattern for this doll quilt is 19. No earlier source of the Mosaic patterns has been found.

Plate 59 Schoolhouse, MG 464

Maker unknown. Circa 1910 • 19″ x 19″
Cotton. Hand-pieced. Machine-quilted diagonally.

House pattern blocks were popular throughout the late 1800s. The *Ladies Art Co.* included three blocks in their original set of blocks published in 1897. Little Red House #373, with the roof and corner outlined in white, is the closest match to this doll quilt. The other house patterns are Jack's House #396, and Old Homestead #108. The fact that *Ladies Art Co.* included three versions in its catalog is strong evidence that they were culling quilt blocks from a variety of publications.

Twentieth-century pattern designers and publishers looked to the *Ladies Art Co.* catalog for block illustrations. A block sent in by Faye Evans of Missouri to *Comfort Magazine* in 1923 was sold as Old Home. Ruth Finley, writing in 1929, called it Little Red Schoolhouse.[20]

Ladies Art Co.

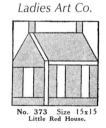

No. 108 Size 13x12
The Old Homestead.

Ladies Art Co.

No. 373 Size 15x15
Little Red House.

Ladies Art Co.

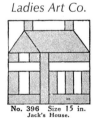

No. 396 Size 15 in.
Jack's House.

Plate 60 Flying Geese, MG 420

Maker unknown. Circa 1900 • 14½″ x 13″ • Cotton. Hand-pieced. Quilted sparsely by hand.

The strip-quilt format decreased in popularity as equal-sized blocks in a grid format became more popular among American quilters in the mid-1800s. *Ladies Art Co.* #94 Wild Goose Chase is a similar pattern, but it has narrower strips and triangles.

Ladies Art Co.

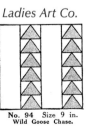

No. 94   Size 9 in.
Wild Goose Chase.

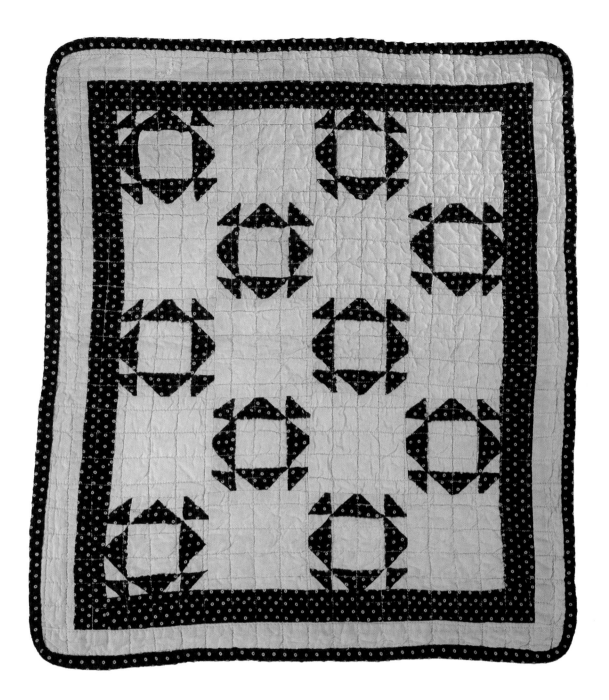

Plate 61 The Cypress, MG 514

Maker unknown. Circa 1900 • 18″ x 15¼″ • Cotton. Hand-pieced. Machine-quilted with ¾″ squares.

The blue and white fabric selections in this quilt suggest a 1890s-1910s date, as these colors were popular at that time. Of course, the pattern might have been revived in the 1930s using fabrics that were in a scrap bag for a long time.

The Cypress pattern, published by the *Kansas City Star* in 1933, is close to the doll-quilt pattern; however, it was designed in three colors to look like a bright red flower on the cypress vine.

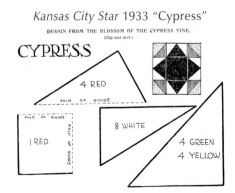

Kansas City Star 1933 "Cypress"

DESIGN FROM THE BLOSSOM OF THE CYPRESS VINE.
(Clip and save.)

CYPRESS

4 RED
FOLD OF GOODS
FOLD OF GOODS
1 RED
FOLD OF GOODS
8 WHITE
4 GREEN
4 YELLOW

Plate 62   Pinwheel, MG 389

Maker unknown. Circa 1880s • 19″ x 17″ • Cotton. Hand-pieced and hand-quilted.

Both The Cypress (see Plate 61) and the Pinwheel quilts are scaled appropriately for a doll bed. Both have inner borders typical of the late 19th and early 20th century adult-size quilts. The double-green print fabrics as well as the pink-striped cottons in this quilt are usually dated to the mid-to-late 1800s, as are the dark-blue and white fabrics in The Cypress.

Ruth Finley in her 1929 book pointed out that this pattern "is made by cutting the four squares of a light four-patch and those of a dark four-patch diagonally across … and then combining the resulting triangles in an alternating color arrangement."[21]

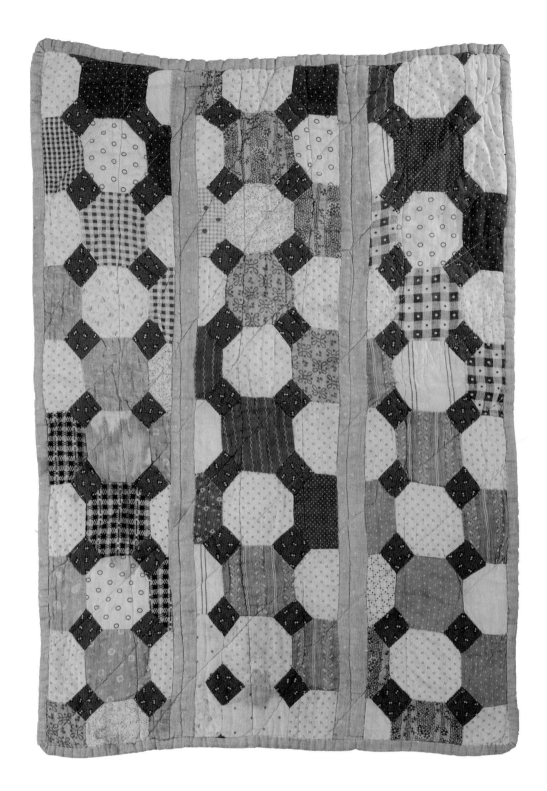

Plate 63 Mosaic Strip, MG 408

Maker unknown. Circa 1900 • 24″ x 17″ • Cotton. Hand-pieced. Machine-quilted sparsely.

The pattern in hexagons and small squares appears to be based on a ceramic-tile design. Tile designs were obvious sources for quilt patterns. This quilt, with its vertical blue stripes, may have been made from pieces of another quilt that were reassembled as a doll quilt. With double-pinks, medium indigo-blue prints, claret prints, and shirting prints, this quilt was likely made at about the turn of the 20th century.

Plate 64 **Four-Patch in Squares**, MG 214

Maker unknown. Circa 1890-1910 • 22″ x 12″ • Cotton. Hand-pieced and hand-quilted. Machine-stitched edging.

Mary: "I like to think that the child who made this quilt was being taught two ways of setting Four-Patch blocks together. Notice the squares are different sizes and the sashing does not line up."

Plate 65 **Square-in-a-Square**, MG 357

Maker unknown. Circa 1900 • 19½″ x 14½″ • Cotton. Hand-pieced. Machine-quilted.

This hodgepodge of quilt pieces that has obviously been constructed quickly makes a delightful doll quilt. Its fabrics include a piece of 1870s brown print, but most are from the late 1800s—polka-dot fabrics, black prints, and white shirting fabric with tiny black widely-spaced printed designs. Mary named the quilt Square-in-a-Square for the diamond pattern block at the bottom half of the quilt.

A young child with a doll, circa
1904-1919.

Virginia Gunn Collection

Turn-of-the-Century Fabrics
(1890s–1910s)

A young girl watches over her doll in a homemade cradle. This circa 1910 photo postcard carries a message about the young girl on the reverse side: "This was your mommie playing nurse when she was a little girl. Keep it. Doesn't she look worried? I bet that baby had a temperature."

Virginia Gunn Collection

Fabrics change with the fashions and the seasons. This was as true a hundred years ago as it is today. Costume historians date fashions by sleeve shape, bodice design, skirt length, and jewelry. When a quilt's pattern and style do not provide enough information to identify the era in which it was made, quilt historians look for clues in the fabrics.

Quilts with dates and known family history become the basis for dating similar quilts with the same fabrics or colors. Dated fabric swatchbooks that salesmen carried are also important tools for dating quilts from the turn of the century.

In addition to doll quilts, Mary also collects doll dresses, obviously for the fabrics they contain. Plates 66, 67, 68, and 69 on the following pages show quilts paired with doll dresses of similar colored fabrics that help date quilts of the 1890s–1910s.

Plate 66 One-Patch Strip, MG 378

Maker unknown. Circa 1880s–1890s • 25″ x 12″ • Cotton. Hand-pieced. Not quilted

The quilt and the dress contain brown calicos of the last quarter of the 19th century. All the quilt fabrics are of a similar grade and quality. They might even be from the same textile mill. Interspersed among the more prominent browns are patches of teal-green stripes, red polka-dots, and a pink check. Brown calicos were fashionable dress fabrics in the decades following the Civil War. This doll quilt probably dates to that period. The backing and separate binding are also tiny brown prints. There is no quilting. The doll quilt lies perfectly flat with no puckers.

Plate 67 **Nine-Patch**, MG 337

Maker unknown. Circa 1890s–1910s • 20″ x 13½″ • Cotton. Hand-pieced and hand-quilted.

The doll dress is made of a black and white print that was marketed at the turn of the century as a "mourning print" (see Glossary). Certainly many women were in mourning in the decades after the Civil War, but the greatest influence was probably England's Queen Victoria in mourning over the death of her husband. Black and white prints were as numerous as brown calicos, but mourning prints entered the marketplace 10 years after the brown calicos.

This doll quilt has two different mourning prints in the top, with one used as the backing fabric. The backing was brought to the front to form a simple binding. With quilting over the entire piece, it was probably made by an adult for a child.

Plate 68 Pinwheel, MG 276

Maker unknown. Circa 1890s–1910s • 22″ x 13″ • Cotton. Hand-pieced. Machine-quilted.

This doll dress has a skirt made of fabric with a printed border. Cotton dress fabrics with printed-lace borders were popular at the turn of the 20th century. Some women cut off the border and discarded it, but others used it in Log Cabin quilts and charm quilts.

The blue fabrics in the quilt are similar medium-blue and dark-indigo with white prints. Black, coral, and red prints are common, too, at this time period. The red fabric in the top left corner, printed with croquet mallets and balls, is a good example of sporting prints which appeared in the 1890s. This quilt has no batting and was quilted minimally by machine.

Plate 69 **Shoo-Fly**, MG 275

Maker unknown. Circa 1900–1920s • 27½″ x 27″
Cotton. Hand-pieced and hand-quilted.

The pink fabrics in this dress and quilt are known as double-pinks. Two shades of pink (or red) are printed one on top of the other to form the traditional pink calico that has appeared in quilts since the early 1800s. Consequently, this fabric alone cannot pinpoint the date of a quilt. With the revived interest in quiltmaking in the early 20th century, quiltmakers desired double-pinks and manufacturers provided them. This well-proportioned quilt with a diamond border is quilted by hand with little hearts near the edges.

Plate 70 Half-Square Triangles, MG 461

Maker unknown. Circa 1890–1900 • 17½" x 15"
Cotton. Hand-pieced. Machine-quilted.

This quilt, with precise piecing of very small triangles, was likely made by an adult. The fabrics it contains are a wide range of prints and colors available after 1890. The neon and black prints in the border are consistent with fabrics popular in this era. Other fabrics are red and black prints, sporting prints with anchors, medium-blue and double-green prints, and many woven checks and plaids. The backing is a dark-blue woven-check fabric that has been brought to the front as binding.

Detail of Half-Square
Triangles showing backing

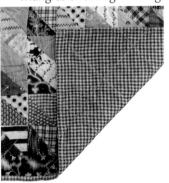

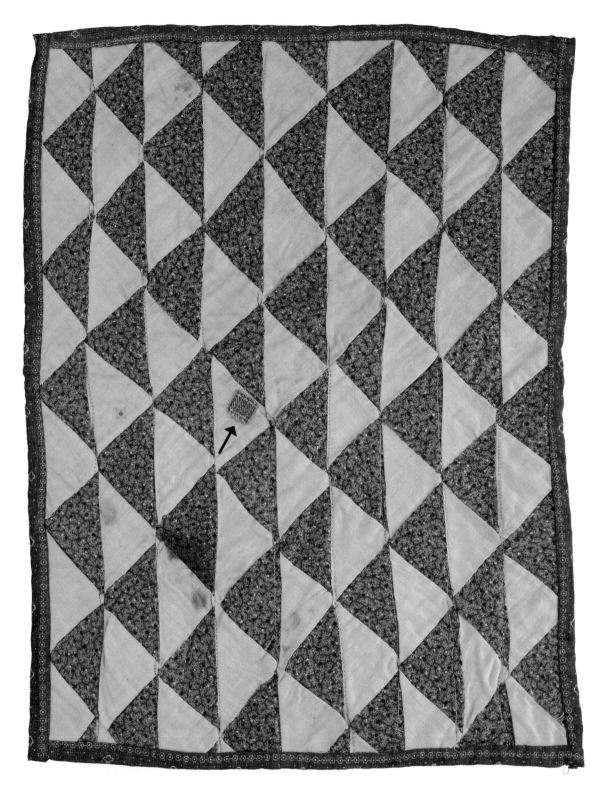

Plate 71 **Pyramids**, MG 387

Maker unknown. 1900-1920s • 15½″ x 11½″ • Cotton. Hand-pieced. Machine-quilted in vertical parallel lines.

The patchwork in this quilt might have been retrieved from a worn-out full-size quilt which itself was made of fabric patched carefully with a tiny brown square of cloth (see arrow). The double-pink fabrics are difficult to date because they were used for a long period of time, but the blue print in the binding dates to the 1900s–1910s.

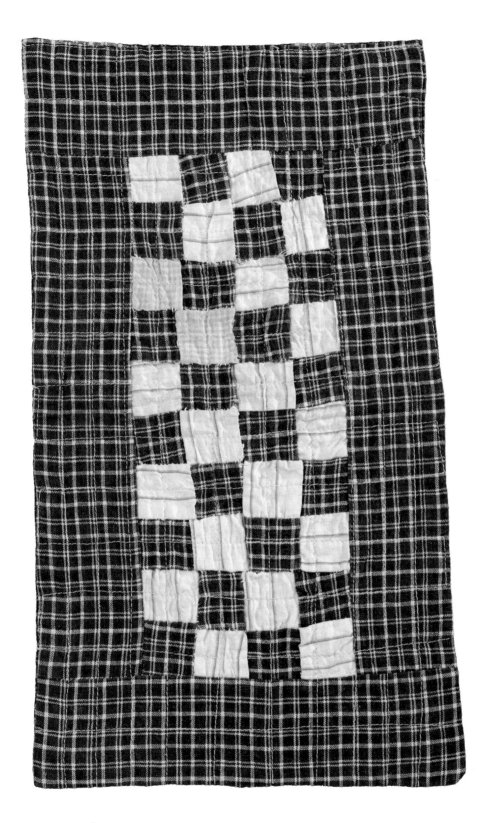

Plate 72 **One-Patch**, MG 462

Maker unknown. Circa 1910s–1920s • 13½″ x 7½″ • Cotton. Hand-pieced. Machine-quilted.

This quilt, with its naïve charm, was probably made by a child and completed by an adult who quilted it on a sewing machine. The top and back layers consist of a woven fabric, sometimes described as "homespun." The backing is brought to the front to bind the quilt.

Plate 73 **Four-Patch**, MG 213

Maker unknown. Circa 1904 • 26½″ x 17½″ • Cotton. Hand-pieced and hand-quilted irregularly. No batting.

A note was attached to this quilt: "Mama made this quilt when six years old in 1904." The fabrics are typical of the 1890-1910 era.

Plate 74 Expanding One-Patch, MG 261

Maker unknown. Circa 1900 • 12" x 9"
Cotton. Hand-pieced and hand-quilted. Machine-stitched around outer edge.

This reversible quilt is full of fabrics from 1900—woven-checked fabric, mourning and shirting prints, double-pinks, and red and white striped fabrics.

Mary: "I could not have made this quilt. I am too programmed to make all the corners meet, all the squares the same size, and all the edges straight."

Detail of Expanding
One-Patch backing

Plate 75 Churn Dash, MG 543

Maker unknown. Circa 1900–1910 • 15″ x 15″ • Cotton. Hand-pieced. Not quilted.

This clean, crisp, red and white quilt made of Turkey-red prints dates from 1900-1910. The single block in the Churn Dash pattern surrounded by a zigzag border makes a striking doll quilt.

Plate 76 Nine-Patch, MG 238

Maker unknown. Circa 1910 • 14½″ x 12″
Cotton. Hand-pieced. Machine-quilted.

Red and white quilts with redwork embroidery date from the 1890s through the 1910s. This cleverly patterned, pieced quilt has no embroidery, but it was likely made in the same time period. Notice how the addition of just one white square at the center of the quilt changes the format from four distinct blocks to one that has a tessellated appearance of red and white crosses. The quilt is backed with another pieced layer.

Detail of Nine-Patch backing

Plate 77 **One-Patch**, MG 470

Maker unknown. Circa 1890s–1910s • 16½″ x 11½″ • Cotton. Hand-pieced and hand-quilted.

    This quilt contains a wide variety of print fabrics including polka-dots on navy-blue, white prints on navy-blue, black on red prints, three different red prints, and six different navy-blue prints. The reverse is made of solid-red cotton. The quilt is precisely pieced, probably by an adult.

Plate 78 **One-Patch**, MG 509

Maker unknown. Circa 1890s–1910s • 19½" x 15½" • Cotton. Hand-pieced and hand-quilted.

The fabrics in this quilt are similar to those in Plate 70 on page 101. They include neon prints, white prints on medium-blue, white prints on navy-blue, star prints, and mourning prints. The backing is gray cotton. The separate binding matches the neon-black fabric in the outer border. It is quilted by hand in diamonds.

Plate 79 One-Patch Wool, MG 78

Maker unknown. Dated 1901 • 16″ x 13″ • Wool and velvet. Hand-pieced and hand-quilted.

This is a rare doll quilt not only for the embroidered date, but also for its fabrics which include wool and velvet. It is hand-quilted with dark thread.

Plate 80 Chimney Sweep, MG 363

Maker unknown. Circa 1910s–1920s • 27" x 16" • Cotton. Hand-pieced. Not quilted.

The palette of red, navy, white, and black in the blocks and border place this quilt squarely in the 1910s. This quilt has no batting and is not quilted.

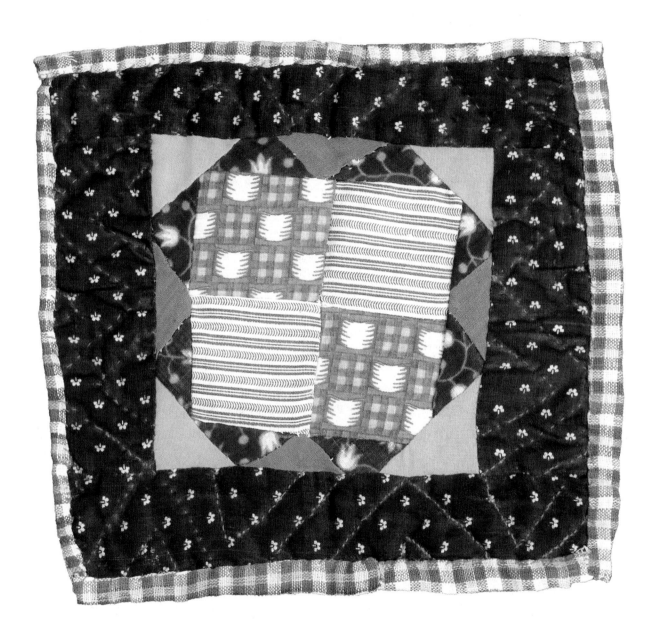

Plate 81 Four-Patch Medallion, MG 325

Maker unknown. Circa 1900-1910 • 8″ x 7½″ • Cotton. Hand-pieced and hand-quilted.

This little quilt gem was probably made by a small child and finished quickly. The big quilting stitches using brown thread and the not-so-straight center medallion are sure signs that a child had her hand in the making of this quilt. The backing is a woven-checked fabric that has been brought to the front for binding purposes. The navy and white prints in the border and the Turkey-red and the chrome-orange fabrics are from the era preceding 1900.

Plate 82 **Four-Patch**, MG 320

Maker unknown. Circa 1890 • 18″ x 18″ • Cotton. Hand-pieced. Not quilted.

   This doll quilt is a single layer with its edges hemmed. There is no batting and therefore no quilting. What makes this quilt interesting is the fabrics it contains. Notice the sporting prints related to horseback riding—horseshoes and bits. The small squares of red and black fabric date from the 1880s and 1890s. The fabrics are thin, making the doll quilt as light as a handkerchief.

A young girl with her doll, circa 1940.

Virginia Gunn Collection

20th-Century Quilts
(1900s-1950s)

A young girl and boy pose
with their doll, circa 1910.

Virginia Gunn Collection

Twentieth-century quilts contrast dramatically with 19th-century quilts. The 20th century began with some Crazy patchwork and redwork embroidery still being done, but the peak of their popularity had passed. Though 20th-century quilts continued to be of the pieced variety, other differences made them markedly different. Fabric choices were much brighter, new patterns emerged, and kits featuring appliqué and pictorial embroidery became popular. Appliqué or pieced patterns with pastel-colored solids served as a counterpoint to the lively print fabrics that were introduced in the 1930s.

In the 1910s, Marie Webster of Marion, Indiana, changed the look and color palette of American quilts. Her quilt designs published in the *Ladies Home Journal* in 1911 and 1912 featured realistic floral designs appliquéd to a white background. Her name became synonymous with quilt history and fine quilt design when she published *Quilts: Their Story and How to Make Them* in 1915. She included color plates of her own quilt designs along with black-and-white photos of antique quilts.

Webster designed a few quilts to appeal to children. The Bedtime Quilt, she wrote, "with its procession of night-clad children will be excellent 'company' for a tot, to whom a story may be told of the birds that sleep in the little trees while the friendly stars keep watch."[22] The blue and white quilt has a rectangular field in the center with white silhouettes of children pointing to the open sky area at the center of the quilt, which is filled with stars and a crescent moon.

Webster's book and her innovative designs inspired other quilt designers to find new sources for inspiration. Ruby McKim, one of the most prolific quilt designers of the early 20th century, used the daily newspaper as her venue for promoting her quilt designs. She was known for her pattern series that offered a different block at least once a week in newspapers nationwide. The "Bible History" and "Colonial History" quilt series were especially designed for children. Each one featured a set of blocks with embroidered vignettes pertaining to a Biblical story or historical event. McKim encouraged mothers to let their children color (rather than embroider) these cloth blocks. At bedtime, parents were to tell their children the stories portrayed on their quilts.

Thread and pattern companies took notice of the continued strong interest in embroidered patterns and produced designs, many of which ended up on quilts made for adults, children, and their dolls. In 1933, the Virginia Snow Studios of Elgin, Illinois, sold "Kiddy Kwilt Stamped Patchwork Blocks" in the following designs: Humpty Dumpty, Duckling, Clown, Goose, and Little Boy Blue at a cost of $1.60 per dozen. The Rainbow

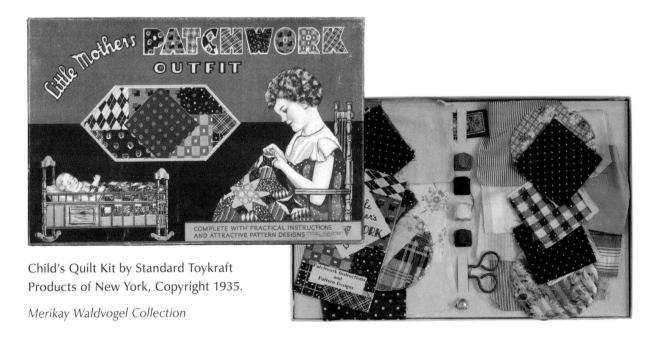

Child's Quilt Kit by Standard Toykraft Products of New York, Copyright 1935.

Merikay Waldvogel Collection

Quilt Block Company of Cleveland, Ohio, sold stamped cloth blocks of Sunbonnet Sue, Dolly Dimple, and Zoo Animals in the early 1930s.

Whereas sewing was essential to 19th-century young women, it was not as important to young girls growing up in the 20th century, but nostalgia played a major role in childhood. Learn-to-sew kits and toy sewing machines were marketed to children. If mothers chose simple patterns, quiltmaking was forgiving and fun. Four-Patch or Nine-Patch quilts nearly always had a positive outcome.

During the 1930s, sewing factories often bundled up their remnants and sold them for specific sewing projects, such as aprons, doll clothes, and quilts. Some companies cut up the fabric remnants on die-cutting machines and sold sets of printed fabric of all one shape. Juvenile-printed cloth designed for children's clothing, curtains, and bedspreads often ended up as backing for a child's quilt (see pages 121 and 122).

Packaged kits for crib quilts with nursery-rhyme themes, farm scenes, and smiling baby animals were sold from the 1930s through the 1950s at department stores and through mail-order catalogs for a small amount of money considering the kit included all the necessary fabric, thread, and instructions. The Teddy Bear doll quilt (see page 123) was actually designed as a pillow to match a kit quilt made in the same pattern.

The first half of the 20th century included two World Wars as well as the best and worst of economic times. A doll, a favorite toy, and a quilt provided the means to escape to a place where everything would be just fine.

Playing hospital in the backyard, circa 1930s.

Virginia Gunn Collection

Plate 83 Embroidered Girl with Hearts, MG 319

Maker unknown. Circa 1910s • 18" x 15" • Cotton. Embroidered and hand-quilted.

Although the young woman in the quilt is sporting a rather dour expression, the borders of embroidered and quilted hearts convey a loving message. The source of this pattern has not been found. Such images would have been sold as transfer patterns printed on light-brown tissue paper. The needle worker would simply heat her iron, put the transfer pattern face down on the cloth, and pass the hot iron over the pattern to transfer the inked image to the cloth. Redwork embroidery, named as such for the non-fading Turkey-red thread, was popular from about 1893 to 1920.

A young girl reads a storybook, with a redwork-embroidered table cover in the foreground, circa 1910.

Merikay Waldvogel Collection

20th-Century Quilts (1900s-1950s) • **119**

Plate 84 Embroidered Animals and People, MG 318

Maker unknown. Circa 1930s • 20½" x 18¼" • Cotton. Embroidered and hand-quilted.

This quilt is filled with embroidered and cross-stitched designs from a variety of sources. All of them were probably specifically designed to appeal to children. Here the quiltmaker has combined them in series as if she might be telling a story or making an album of a particular child's favorite things.

The published sources of the patterns have not been found. The Japanese girl and the Little Dutch Boy were popular images in the 1910s-1930s, as were the butterfly, blue bird, baby chicks, and swan.

Plate 85 Jemima Puddle-Duck, MG 447

Maker unknown. Circa 1920s • 19½" x 13" • Cotton. Embroidered and hand-quilted.

This image comes from the *Tale of Jemima Puddle-Duck* published in 1908 by British author Beatrix Potter. A prolific author and artist, she oversaw the production and design of her books illustrated with her own watercolor images. An entire industry grew up around her characters.[23]

This particular outline embroidery design of Jemima Puddle-Duck was published in 1920 in the women's magazine, *Pictorial Review*, on a sheet of 11 transfer patterns titled Simple Designs That Little Miss Can Embroider or Paint. The editors suggested a variety of uses for the patterns: "These motifs can be applied to children's bibs, aprons, bonnets, and other articles of apparel. A pretty tray doily to slip under a child's plate could be of oilcloth, painting birds or geese in bright colors. If designs are embroidered, outline, chain, long-and-short stitches may be used."[24]

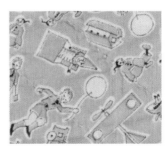

Detail of Jemima
Puddle-Duck backing

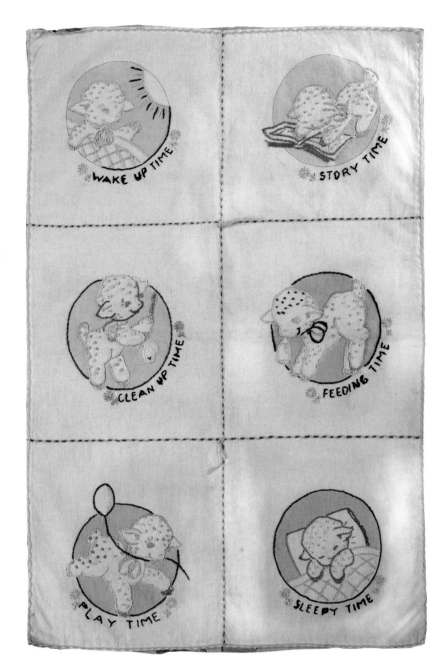

Detail of Lambs backing

Plate 86 Lambs, MG 508

Maker unknown. Circa 1932 • 23½" x 15½" • Cotton. Embroidered and tied.

This quilt was made of a set of stamped and tinted blocks sold by Vogart Inc. Though numbered #565, the set is not named on the selvedge printing. The manufacturer, Vogart Inc., was identified based on a catalog advertisement.

The mail-order needlework company W. L. M. Clark, Inc. of St. Louis, Missouri, advertised similar stamped and tinted cloth blocks in 1937. Their Scottie Quilt was described as "a pet quilt for any child—dogs tinted in deep gray with red ribbons."[25] Another was Tabby's Day, described as "a quilt any little boy or girl will love."[26] The set of eight cloth blocks with instructions cost just 30 cents.

The quilt lining on this particular quilt is a colorful graphic rendering of children dressed up and marching in a parade.

POPULAR TEDDY BEAR QUILT

Plate 87 Teddy Bear, MG 450

Maker unknown. Circa 1960 • 16½″ x 16″
Cotton. Appliquéd, embroidered, and quilted by hand.

   This doll quilt is made from a pillow kit designed to match
a center medallion crib quilt named Teddy Bear. The quilt kit
appeared as early as 1951, but the pillow kit did not appear until
the 1961-62 *Herrschner*'s catalog. The Teddy Bear quilt kit cost $1.98
for the crib size and $2.98 for the single-bed size. The pillow kit
cost 98 cents plus 20 cents for thread.[27]

Plate 88 Grandmother's Flower Garden, MG 217

Maker unknown. Circa 1935 • 16½″ x 13″ • Cotton. Hand-pieced and hand-quilted.

Grandmother's Flower Garden has become a classic American quilt design. It dates back to the 1830s when Hexagon Mosaic quilts in rich earth-toned chintz fabrics were the fashion. During the mid-20th century, the pattern was revived in bright colors and named Flower Garden, Grandmother's Flower Garden, and Nosegay. The quilt is not easy to construct, especially finishing the irregular outer edges. Therefore, an adult probably made this quilt for a child.

Plate 89 Nine-Patch Scrap, MG 362

Maker unknown. Circa 1935 • 20" x 13" • Cotton. Hand-pieced and hand-quilted. Machine-bound.

Mary's mother was told that every girl should make a Nine-Patch by the time she was nine years old. This one is simple yet effective when alternating the print squares with solid-colored blocks in the bright colors of typical 1930s fabrics.

Plate 90 **Trip Around the World**, MG 287

Maker unknown. Circa 1935 • 21½″ x 17½″ • Cotton. Hand-pieced. Machine stitched at edge. Not quilted.

Mary: "Now see! That's a quilt made by an adult for a child with love. I can't imagine a child making something that is so complicated to piece."

Doris Mulonek

Mary Ghormley Collection

Plate 91 **Brick Wall Quilt and Pillow**, MG 184

Made by Doris Mulonek, Crete, Nebraska. Circa 1935 • 9½" x 9½"
Wool. Machine-pieced and tied with wool yarn.

    This is a reversible quilt made of wool suiting fabric. The edge is bound in a blanket stitch with red yarn. The attached velvet pillow fringed in lace has an embroidered flower or tree with pink pompoms. Both are obviously made by a child. A search of early 20th-century census data identified Doris Mulonek as the young quilter who made this. (See Doris Mulonek's story on pages 19-20.)

Plate 92 One-Patch, MG 253

Made by Nell Botkin Ghormley (1888-1956) Circa 1950
20″ x 13″ • Cotton. Hand-pieced. Machine-quilted.

This quilt was made by Roger Ghormley's mother for her granddaughters, Peggy, Phyllis, and Marilyn Ghormley around 1950. The colors and prints are typical of the 1950s—teal green, bright red, navy and white stripes, and lavender floral prints on a white background. The backing is a printed plaid. The quilt is quilted by machine in a square diamond design.

Nell Botkin Ghormley

Roger Ghormley Collection

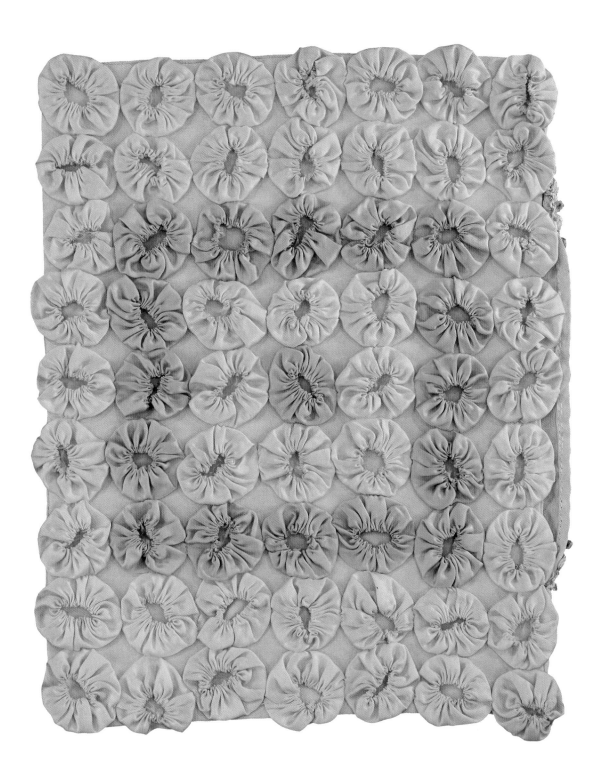

Plate 93 **Yo-Yo**, MG 427

Maker unknown. Circa 1920–1930s • 11¾″ x 10¼″ • Taffeta. Gathered and hand-stitched.

    Yo-Yo quilts are not, strictly speaking, quilts since they do not have two layers quilted together. Instead, small gathered rosettes or Yo-Yo's are tacked to each other and then tacked to a lining fabric that is visible through the web of Yo-Yo's. The choice of this peach-colored taffeta makes this a sophisticated doll quilt. Adult-size quilts in this color and style were called "*Boudoir*" quilts and date from the 1920s.

Photography by W. A. Williams,
Newark, New Jersey, circa 1880s-1890s.

Virginia Gunn Collection

Conclusion

A young girl and her doll, circa 1904-1918.

Virginia Gunn Collection

Doll quilts are little gems—microcosms of quilt history. They haven't been studied in depth before, which is unfortunate because they often contain hundreds of pieces of rarely-seen fabrics. Accurately dating doll quilts is difficult so collectors often pass them by, afraid to take a chance. Mary Ghormley was initially drawn to the naïve charm of the doll quilts, but found herself even more enthralled by the fabrics they contained.

As we have shown, most doll quilts do not carry sufficient information to track down the name of the maker or even what area of the country she lived in. But by examining the quilts closely, and by using what information has been written on the evolution of quilt styles, patterns, color choices, and fabrics, we come close to supplying pieces of the missing information, especially as to when the quilts were made.

Mary's doll-quilt collection, selections of which are included in this book, covers more than 100 years of quilt history. Once we know the age of the fabrics in the doll quilt, we can begin to imagine the accompanying details: a child growing up in a Federal Style home in Philadelphia in the

Two girls with their dolls, circa 1904-1918.

Virginia Gunn Collection

early 1800s, or a young girl playing house under a shade tree of a two-story white-frame house in a small town in Indiana in the early 1900s.

Many of the doll quilts in this book are not perfectly constructed. They are often made of partially-finished quilt blocks and machine-stitched quickly. Yet, therein lies the charm of these quilts. Examining them closely, one can almost imagine the setting of these spur-of-the-moment projects: an impatient child wanting the doll quilt quickly and begging to put in a few stitches herself.

Until recently, doll quilts have not been valued as antiques. After heavy use and frequent washings, they are rarely in mint condition when found. Since few doll quilts are dated and initialed, the provenance (or known history) of the doll quilts is hard to determine. Their haphazard designs and quirky constructions also have placed them in a less-than-desirable collecting category.

That being said, as long-time quilt collectors, Mary and I are strong advocates for doll quilts—the quirkier, the better. If you have them in your family, record the memories of the doll and its quilt. If you are fortunate to have a young child in your life, make a doll quilt with him or her. And, if you see one in an antique store, consider giving it a home. We hope we have opened your eyes and hearts to these small wonders.

Endnotes

1 *A New England Girlhood* (Gloucester, MA: Peter Smith, 1973. First published in 1889.) Quoted in Mirra Bank *Anonymous Was a Woman* (New York: St. Martin's Press, 1979), 23.

2 See Christiane Fischer, *Let Them Speak for Themselves: Women in the American West, 1849 to 1900* (Hamden, CT: Archon Books, 1977) page 288.

3 See Catherine E. Beecher, *Treatise on the Domestic Economy for the Use of Young Ladies At Home and At School* (New York: Harper & Brothers, 1858), 324.

4 *A New England Girlhood*, 122-124. Quoted in Bruce Johnson, *A Child's Comfort* (New York: The Museum of American Folk Art, 1977), 13.

5 For a photo of three-year-old Belle, see Patricia Cox Crews and Ronald C. Naugle (eds.), *Nebraska Quilts and Quiltmakers* (Lincoln, NE: University of Nebraska Press, 1991), 56.

6 See *No Time on My Hands: As Told to Nellie S. Yost* (Caldwell, ID: Coxton Printers, 1963, 335-336; Lincoln, NE: University of Nebraska Press, 1986).

7 See Bets Ramsey and Merikay Waldvogel, *Quilts of Tennessee: Images of Domestic Life Prior to 1930* (Nashville: Rutledge Hill Press, 1986), 90.

8 Ibid., 91.

9 See Diane Fagan Affleck, *Just New From the Mills: Printed Cottons in America* (North Andover, MA: Museum of American Textile History, 1987), 11.

10 Diane Fagan Affleck, email communication to author, 13 December 2006.

11 See Deborah E. Kraak, "19th-Century American Printed Patchwork and Japonisme," *CIETA Bulletin* 80, 2003, 87.

12 See Fannie Williams, "Linda's Crazy Quilt," *Golden Days for Boys and Girls* (May 21, 1887): 1, 386-7.

13 *Hearth and Home*, March 1895.

14 Ibid., June 1901.

15 Ibid., September 1903.

16 *The Household*, October 1881.

17 Ibid., November 1881.

18 *Hearth and Home*, September 1901.

19 See Ruth Finley, *Old Patchwork Quilts and the Women Who Made Them* (Reprinted by McLean, VA: EPM Publications, 1992), 114-115.

20 Ibid., 196.

21 Ibid., 56.

22 See Marie Webster, *Quilts: Their Story and How to Make Them* (Garden City, New York: Doubleday, Page & Co., 1915), 26.

23 See Judy Taylor, et al., *Beatrix Potter 1866-1943: The Artist and Her World* (London: The Penguin Group, 1987), 132-136.

24 See Deborah Harding, *Red and White: American Redwork Quilts and Patterns* (New York: Rizzoli International Press, 2000), 122.

25 See *Woman's World*, November 1937, 24.

26 See *Home Arts Needlecraft*, September 1937, 21.

27 *Herrschner's* 85 (Chicago: Herrschners, 1961), 16.

Suggested Readings

Affleck, Diane L. Fagan. *Just New From the Mills: Printed Cottons in America*. North Andover, MA: Museum of American Textile History, 1987.

Aug, Bobbie. "At Mother's Knee: Collecting Early Doll Quilts." *McCall's Quilting Vintage Quilts* (Spring 2002): 22-23.

Carrick, Alice Van Leer. "Old Dolls and Their Furniture." *Collector's Luck*. Boston: Atlantic Monthly Press, 1919: 194-207.

Fox, Sandi. *Small Endearments: Nineteenth-Century Quilts for Children and Dolls*. Nashville: Rutledge Hill Press, 1994.

Ghormley, Mary. "Pint-Size Patchwork." *Quilter's Newsletter Magazine* No. 363 (June 2004): 30-33.

Gunn, Virginia. "Dress Fabrics of the Late 19th Century: Their Relationship to Period Quilts." *Bits and Pieces/Textile Traditions*, ed. Jeannette Lasansky. Lewisburg, PA: Oral Traditions Project, 1991: 4-15.

Johnson, Bruce. *A Child's Comfort: Baby and Doll Quilts in American Folk Art*. New York: Harcourt Brace Jovanovich with the Museum of American Folk Art, 1977.

Kiracofe, Roderick. *The American Quilt*. New York: Clarkson Potter, 1993: 111-113.

Lavitt, Wendy. *American Folk Dolls*. New York: Alfred A. Knopf, 1982.

Levie, Eleanor. *Great Little Quilts: 45 Antique Crib and Doll-Size Quilts*. New York: Harry Abrams, 1990.

Lobdell, Heather Wright. "Half-Pint Patchwork." *Country Home* (February 1994): 68-73.

Long, Pat and Dennis Duke. "Baby, Crib and Doll Quilts." *America's Glorious Quilts*. New York: Hugh Lauter Levin, 1987: 176-191.

Martin, Nancy. *Decorate with Quilts and Collections*. Bothell, WA: That Patchwork Place, 1996: 179.

Pellman, Rachel and Kenneth Pellman. *Amish Doll Quilts, Dolls, and Other Playthings*. Intercourse, PA: Good Books, 1986.

Quilts: The Fabric of Friendship. York, PA: The York County Heritage Trust, 2000: 115-124.

Smith, Wilene. "Quilt History in Old Periodicals: A New Interpretation." *Uncoverings 1990*, ed. Sally Garoutte. San Francisco: American Quilt Study Group, 1991: 188-213.

Thompson, Shirley. *Think Small*. Edmonds, WA: Powell Publications, 1990.

Tracy, Kathleen. *American Doll Quilts: 16 Little Projects That Honor a Tradition*. Woodinville, WA: That Patchwork Place, 2004.

Woodard, Thomas K. and Blanche Greenstein. *Crib Quilts and Other Small Wonders*. New York: Bonanza Books, 1988. First published in 1981.

Glossary

Appliqué: laid-on pieces of cloth sewn to a contrasting background material.

Backing: the fabric used as the underside of a quilt; also called a lining.

Bar quilts: quilts made of narrow strips of cloth set side by side that extend the full length of the quilt; also called Strip quilts.

Batting: the middle layer of a quilt, traditionally made of cotton, wool, or polyester.

Binding: the finish treatment for the raw outer edges of a quilt, done quickly by folding the back fabric to the front or vice versa. A slightly more complicated method is to enclose the raw edges by sewing a strip of straight or bias material to the quilt's four sides.

Block: a unit or section of a quilt top; it may be appliquéd, embroidered, pieced, or a combination of techniques.

Border: a band of cloth that frames the outer edge of the quilt or surrounds a center medallion. The border may be appliquéd, pieced, or a combination of techniques.

Charm quilt: a quilt in which every piece is cut from a different piece of fabric. The block used is a simple shape—a hexagon, diamond, or triangle. Searching for sufficient fabrics becomes a challenge.

Chintz: a Hindi term (dating from 1614) describing exotic, painted, and printed calico cotton fabrics imported from India. Chintz fabric was often used for bed hangings, draperies, and upholstery.

Center medallion: a large central motif, typically a circle, oval, diamond, or star, surrounded by successive units or borders.

Comfort: a tied (knotted) quilt; rather than lines of stitching to hold the quilt layers together, the layers are tied and knotted with string at regular intervals over the quilt top. Also called a comforter.

Coverlet: a bed covering, usually not quilted.

Crazy-piecing: irregular shapes of cloth sewn to a cloth square, which is then joined to other similarly-constructed blocks to form a quilt top; fabric shapes often are embellished with embroidery stitching.

Embroidery: decorative stitching that embellishes and enhances quilt designs.

English paper-piecing: a method of hand-piecing in which fabric shapes are basted over paper templates and whip-stitched together along their fabric edges. Hexagon mosaic quilts were commonly made in this manner in England in the early 1800s.

Foundation-piecing: assembling a block by sewing pieces to a foundation of muslin or plain fabric, thereby adding strength and stability to delicate or stretchy fabrics.

Homespun fabrics: woven fabric that has the appearance of home-produced fabrics that required spinning and weaving.

Log Cabin: a type of quilt pattern in which narrow fabric strips, or "logs," are added one at a time in succession around a small center square. The sequence of adding light and dark "logs" creates a distinctive pattern when the blocks are joined together to form a top.

Madder prints: cloth that was dyed using a vegetable dye until it was replaced by a synthetic dye in the late 19th century. The madder prints ranged from red to purple as well as rust, orange, and dark brown.

Medallion quilt: a type of quilt in which a central motif, surrounded by multiple borders, serves as the focal point.

Mourning prints: decorative designs printed in black on white cotton marketed for women in mourning.

Ombre prints: cloth printed in soft gradations from dark to light; also known as fondue prints.

Pieced work: joining pieces of cloth together to form quilt blocks, usually creating geometric designs.

Quilt: two layers of cloth with padding between, stitched or tied together.

Quilting: in general, the process of making a quilt; specifically, the process of making small stitches that hold the three layers of a quilt together.

Redwork embroidery: embroidery using red thread only; popular in the 1890s-1910s on dresser scarves, hand towels, and quilts.

Roller printing: a technique of printing fabric using engraved metal cylinders.

Set: the arrangement of blocks in a quilt-top design.

Shirting prints: a sparsely-printed white-cotton fabric popularly used in shirtwaist dresses of the early 20th century.

Sporting prints: print fabric popular at the end of the 19th century that featured popular sports of the day, such as baseballs and bats, anchors and ship's wheels, horseshoes and bits.

String-piecing: the joining of narrow strips of fabric, usually in random size, to make a quilt block.

Strip quilts: *see Bar quilts*

Template-piecing: *see English paper-piecing*

Tesselation: the careful interlocking of shapes in a pattern as in a mosaic tile floor.

Top: the upper and outer layer of a quilt.

Turkey-red prints: fabric printed in a color-fast red dye which originated in the country of Turkey. Years later, when other countries perfected the process, the true-red color-fast fabric was still referred to as Turkey-red.

White-work quilts: a type of quilt with a top of solid-white cloth, usually featuring elaborately quilted and stuffed designs.

Whole cloth: a type of quilt with a top of solid or figured material, often three panels seamed together and quilted simply.

Index

album quilt, 120

appliqué, 12, 15, 33, 117, 123

Bars, 14, 25, 31

Beatrix Potter, 16, 121

Brick Wall Quilt and Pillow, 19, 127

Broken Dishes, 39

Brown Goose, 81

calico, 12-13, 43-44, 77, 81, 97-98, 100

Carolina Lily, 15, 33

charm quilt, 99

Chimney Sweep, 111

chintz, 5, 24, 27, 33, 36, 124

Churn Dash, 82, 106

Cocheco Printworks, 52, 54, 62

comforts, 43

Crazy, 6, 15, 20-21, 54, 58-73, 116

crepe, 70, 72

Cypress, 89-90

Diamonds, 14, 16-17, 25, 28, 32, 34, 83, 93, 100, 109, 128

double-green prints, 51, 53, 55, 90, 101

double-pink prints, 30, 35, 51, 53, 57, 80, 85, 91, 100, 102, 105

Double T Square, 83

Embroidered Animal and People, 120

Embroidered Girl with Hearts, 119

embroidery, 16, 20, 58, 60-61, 64, 70, 107, 110, 116-117, 119-123, 127

English paper templates, 28

Evening Star, 25, 31

Flying Geese, 35, 88

Four-Patch, 6, 13, 25, 27, 43, 46, 53, 55, 90, 92, 104, 112-113, 118

Gee's Bend, Alabama, 46

Grandmother's Flower Garden, 124

Half-Square Triangles, 14, 101

Hit-or-Miss, 52

homespun fabrics, 103

Hour Glass, 28, 65, 86

Jemima Puddle-Duck, 121

kit quilts, 6, 117-118, 123

lace, 54, 60-61, 64, 99, 127

Lambs, 122

LeMoyne Star, 26, 32

Log Cabin, 43, 45-50, 54, 99

madder prints, 30, 43, 57, 65

Medallion, 5, 29, 85, 112, 123

Mill Wheel, 17

mosaic, 25, 86, 124

Mosaic Strip, 91

Mother Goose, 16

mourning prints, 65-66, 79, 98, 105, 109

muslin, 67, 71

Nine-Patch, 6, 13, 25-26, 35, 38, 43, 56, 98, 107, 118, 125

ombre prints, 24, 31

One-Patch, 13, 18, 20, 25, 36-37, 97, 103, 105, 108-110, 128

paisley, 32, 51-52, 62

Pinwheel, 39, 90, 99

plaid, 67, 70, 85, 101, 128

polka-dots, 66, 82, 93, 97, 108

Pyramids, 102

rayon, 70, 72

redwork embroidery, 16, 107, 116, 119

roller-printed fabrics, 24, 28, 31, 33

Sawtooth Star, 43, 57, 86

Schoolhouse, 87

sewing sampler, 13

shirting prints, 65, 67, 82, 91, 93, 105

silk, 61, 68, 70, 72

Shoo-Fly, 100

Sixteen-Patch, 51

sporting prints, 99, 100, 113

Square-in-a-Square, 18, 93

Sugar Loaf, 79

taffeta, 60-61, 129

T quilt, 80

Teddy Bear, 118, 123

Trip Around the World, 126

velvet, 60-61, 70, 110, 127

Whole Cloth, 14-15, 24-25, 29, 54

Wool, 45, 55, 58, 61, 77, 110, 127

woven fabrics, 25, 27, 44, 51, 66-67, 70, 80, 101, 103, 105, 112

Yo-Yo, 129

About the International Quilt Study Center & Museum

The International Quilt Study Center was established in 1997 at the University of Nebraska-Lincoln to encourage the interdisciplinary study of all aspects of quiltmaking and to foster preservation of this tradition. The Center's mission is to collect, preserve, study, exhibit, and promote discovery of quilts and quiltmaking traditions from many cultures, countries, and time periods.

The International Quilt Study Center & Museum is a dynamic center of formal and informal learning and discovery for students, teachers, scholars, artists, quilters, and others within and outside the University. Its comprehensive, worldwide, and accessible collection of quilts, related textiles, and documents serves as a primary text for study, insight and inspiration.

Collections

The collections of the International Quilt Study Center have grown to include more than 2,300 quilts representing more than twenty countries, including significant collections of African American and Pennsylvania Amish quilts, and contemporary studio art quilts, as well as antique quilts spanning four centuries. The IQSC is dedicated to locating the finest examples of quilts of all eras and geographical origins. The ongoing commitment to assembling this richly diverse and fascinating resource has led to many exciting discoveries of quilts and textiles to add to the collection.

Academic Center

In conjunction with establishment of the center, the University of Nebraska-Lincoln established a one-of-a-kind graduate program in Textile History with an emphasis in Quilt Studies. This unique program, part of the Department of Textiles, Clothing and Design, was first offered in 2001.

Public Exhibitions

To date, the International Quilt Study Center has organized over 20 comprehensive quilt exhibitions which have traveled to more than 50 locations throughout the United States and internationally.

About the Author

Merikay Waldvogel is a nationally known quilt authority. Her interest in quilts dates back to the mid-1970s when she purchased one out-of-the-ordinary quilt in Chicago, Illinois, where she was living at the time. As her collection grew, she began to ask questions about the fabrics and patterns in quilts in order to learn more about the quilts' histories.

Since then she has written several books, including *Quilts of Tennessee: Images of Domestic Life Prior to 1930*; *Soft Covers for Hard Times: Quiltmaking and the Great Depression*; *Patchwork Souvenirs of the 1933 Chicago World's Fair*; and *Southern Quilts: Surviving Relics of the Civil War*.

She has served on the Board of Directors of the American Quilt Study Group and the Alliance for American Quilts. She is a Research Fellow at the International Quilt Study Center at the University of Nebraska-Lincoln, where she has frequently lectured and conducted classes.

She was raised in the Midwest and currently resides in Knoxville, Tennessee, with her retired husband, Jerry Ledbetter. In addition to quilts, she enjoys bike-riding, hiking in the Smoky Mountains, and traveling.

She has a B.A. in French from Monmouth College in Illinois and an M.A. in Linguistics from the University of Michigan.

About the Collector

Mary Ghormley of Lincoln, Nebraska, has been making quilts since the 1950s. She is a founder, past president, and life member of the Lincoln Quilters Guild. In 1987 she was elected to the Nebraska Quilter's Hall of Fame, in recognition of the many roles she has served in the renaissance of quiltmaking and collecting in the late 20th century.

In the 1970s, she taught quilting during the quilt revival of that decade. In the 1980s she helped document quilts for the Nebraska Quilt Project survey and is pictured in the book *Nebraska Quilts and Quiltmakers*. Since its formation in 1997, she has volunteered at the International Quilt Study Center at the University of Nebraska-Lincoln.

A number of full-size and doll-size quilts collected and made by Mary have been acquired by the International Quilt Study Center. The Center also has acquired her library of quilt books which will be housed in the Mary Campbell Ghormley Reading Room in the new home for the International Quilt Study Center & Museum scheduled to open in March 2008.

Mary has been married 64 years to Roger Ghormley. They have five grown children, eighteen grandchildren, and seven great-grandchildren.